Management and Industrial Relations Series

2

Tackling discrimination at the workplace

Management and Industrial Relations Series

Edited for the Social Science Research Council by

DOROTHY WEDDERBURN
Principal of Bedford College, London

MICHAEL BROMWICH
Professor of Finance and Accounting, University of Reading

and

DOUGLAS BROOKS
Director, Walker Brooks and Partners

Social science research has much to contribute to the better understanding and solution of problems in the field of management and industrial relations. The difficulty, however, is that there is frequently a gap between the researcher and the practitioner who wants to use the research results. This new series is designed to make available to practitioners in the relevant fields the results of the best research which the Social Science Research Council (SSRC) has supported in the fields of management and industrial relations. The subjects covered and the style adopted will appeal to managers, trade unionists and administrators because there will be an emphasis upon the practical implifications of research findings. But the volumes will also serve as a useful introduction to particular areas for students and teachers of management and industrial relations.

The series is jointly produced by the Cambridge University Press and the Social Science Research Council.

Other books in the series
1. *Lost managers : supervisors in industry and society* by JOHN CHILD and BRUCE PARTRIDGE
2. *Tackling discrimination at the workplace : an analysis of sex discrimination in Britain* by BRIAN CHIPLIN and PETER J. SLOANE
3. *Inflation accounting : an introduction to the debate* by GEOFFREY WHITTINGTON

Tackling discrimination at the workplace

An analysis of sex discrimination in Britain

by
BRIAN CHIPLIN
and
PETER J. SLOANE

CAMBRIDGE UNIVERSITY PRESS

Cambridge
London New York New Rochelle
Melbourne Sydney

Published by the Press Syndicate of the University of Cambridge
The Pitt Building, Trumpington Street, Cambridge CB2 1RP
32 East 57th Street, New York, NY 10022, USA
296 Beaconsfield Parade, Middle Park, Melbourne 3206, Australia

First published 1982

Printed in Great Britain at
the University Press, Cambridge

Library of Congress catalogue card number: 82-4384

British Library Cataloguing in Publication Data

Chiplin, Brian
Tackling discrimination at the workplace.
– (Management and industrial relations series; 2)
1. Women – Employment – Great Britain
I. Title   II. Sloane, Peter J.
III. Series
331.4′133′0941   HD6137

ISBN 0 521 24565 6 hard covers
ISBN 0 521 28788 X paperback

Contents

Preface

The research, the results of which are presented in this book, originated in a project entitled 'Discrimination and the employment of females', which was supported by the Social Science Research Council over the period 1974–7 at the University of Nottingham. During this period one of the two investigators, P. J. Sloane, took up the post of Professor of Economics and Management at Paisley College. However, the above award was supplemented by a grant from the Manpower Services Commission and The Training Services Agency, which enabled the fieldwork to be extended from the East Midlands to the West of Scotland. A final report to the s.s.r.c. on the project (HR 2904/1) was lodged in the British Library at the end of 1978, but some further analysis has continued since that date, as indicated in the list of publications associated with the project which appears at the end of the book.

The authors wish to acknowledge the research assistance, particularly in relation to Chapter 6, of M. Curran, A. Reynolds and C. J. Parsley at Nottingham and also the work of W. S. Siebert who acted as research fellow at Paisley. K. Miller of the University of Strathclyde Law School kindly commented on the legal aspects of Chapter 4, although any errors and omissions must remain the responsibility of the authors. We are also indebted to numerous individuals in a range of organisations without whose willing co-operation the research would have foundered at an early stage. Finally, we are grateful to Professors Dorothy Wedderburn and Michael Bromwich and Mr Douglas Brooks for commenting on an earlier version of the manuscript, to Jean Craft for typing assistance and to Geoffrey Hillier for mending the word processor.

B.C. and P.J.S.
September 1981

vii

1
Introduction

Unequal pay and opportunities at work are widespread but the causes are complex and not simply to be explained by 'discrimination' at work, by either employers or employees. Following growing public awareness of these issues, fuelled by various women's pressure groups, legislation was passed in Britain in 1970 (the Equal Pay Act) and 1975 (the Sex Discrimination Act), and an Equal Opportunities Commission was set up in order to improve the relative position of women at work. It is important initially to determine how much of the gross difference in male and female earnings can be attributed to discrimination. This in turn implies that we must attempt to measure discrimination, and economists have made considerable efforts to do just this.

If we can obtain sound estimates of the degree of discrimination experienced by women we can make some judgement as to how far the relative position of women in the labour market is likely to be influenced by the above legislation, recognising that legislation may be important not only in terms of its direct impact but also in terms of its influence in shaping attitudes. In this context it is useful to consider the experience of the United States where equal-opportunities legislation has been in force longer than in Britain and also is more extensive in terms, for instance, of its affirmative action provisions, which require certain firms to set goals and timetables for increasing the employment of minority workers (including women) in the various job levels of the organisation. Legal intervention in the United States has indeed led to fairly extensive attempts to measure discrimination within organisations using a similar methodology to that adopted in this book. Broadly speaking, studies in both the United States and Britain[1] have found sex discrimination in earnings in the order of 10 per cent – that is women earn 10 per cent less than men simply because they are women. This

1

figure is roughly a quarter of the total difference in earnings between men and women, which may have the implication that changes in attitudes to family and labour-market roles may be more important than legislation in closing the gap in earnings between the sexes.

In analysing the reasons for earnings differentials by gender we may distinguish between factors which influence the supply side and those which operate on the demand side of the labour market. Thus, in the former case, differences between the sexes in education, skill and motivation may give rise to differences in occupational and industrial distributions, and consequently in earnings, which are not directly caused by the behaviour of employers or employees. In the same firm, and within the same occupation, earnings can vary as productivity, hours and effort vary, where income is directly related to such factors. Surprisingly few attempts have been made to measure the relative performance (output per worker per time period) of the sexes when engaged on comparable tasks. However, one such study by Battalio, Kagel and Reynolds, based on an experimental economy established at the Addiction Research Foundation in Ontario, Canada,[2] found that although female earnings were about 75 per cent of male earnings such a difference could not be explained by discrimination but was related entirely to differential productivity (i.e. output of woven woollen belts on small portable handlooms). This indicates the importance of taking into account supply-side characteristics of the workers concerned. On the other hand, the employment distribution and earnings levels may be influenced by the attitudes of employers or male workers. In general it is assumed that discrimination manifests itself on the demand side of the market but it has to be recognised that, even if such discrimination is removed, supply-side differences may still leave substantial inequalities in the earnings and employment distributions. However, if discrimination is practised it may have feedback effects on the incentive to acquire skills and other valued characteristics. Thus supply-side factors do not operate independently of discrimination. In addition, there are forms of discrimination which occur prior to the individual's employment, such as access to educational opportunities and general role stereotyping. It is for these reasons that analysis of the discriminatory component of earnings differentials is so difficult and why we suggest in Chapter 5 that it is important to analyse specific decisions which may throw light on the wider problem.

Introduction

In broad terms one can suggest the following 'reasons', or combination of reasons, why women on average might have lower earnings than men: (i) they may have fewer opportunities to receive education and training than men; (ii) they may have less-well-paid jobs than men for given levels of qualifications, experience and other personal characteristics; (iii) they may receive lower pay given the job, which could amount to wage discrimination if the jobs being compared are sufficiently similar.

In considering these differences we must take into account the effects not only of gender but also of family responsibilities and their associated implications for motivation, reliability and willingness to accept promotion to more demanding work tasks.

We consider such factors further in Chapter 3, where we examine the overall male–female earnings differential in the U.K. However, legislation on equal pay and equal opportunity is primarily directed at the level of the individual organisation and this is the main focus of the book as a whole. In Chapter 2 an attempt is made to sort out exactly what is meant by discrimination from the perspective of economic analysis, to analyse the main motives and explanations for discriminatory behaviour, and to provide comparisons and contrasts with legal interpretations embodied in the main provisions of British law. The precise way in which the law has been interpreted by the courts is considered in Chapter 4. Further, the new proposed Code of Practice published by the Equal Opportunities Commission does suggest that firms and other organisations should conduct a detailed appraisal of their practices in relation to discrimination and the role of women within their employment; and we examine how firms might seek to implement these provisions of the code. In Chapter 5 we outline many of the problems involved and illustrate the sort of procedures that are necessary if such an appraisal is to be meaningful. The discussion is continued in Chapter 6, where the point is made that attention should be paid to recruitment and promotion, as it is through these mechanisms that current practices and attitudes are most readily ascertained. By means of a case study, we show that it is possible to attempt to isolate any discriminatory component in the decisions involved. Finally, the policy implications of the analysis are detailed in the concluding Chapter 7.

2
Economic and legal perspectives on discrimination

It is important to be clear about what we mean when we use the term 'discrimination', which may refer to a number of distinct, if related, forms of behaviour. First, we must consider the approach of the economist. Neo-classical economists tend to think of discrimination as a kind of commodity for which, like any other, a price has to be paid, in this case in the form of lower income. On the other hand, radical economists tend to see discrimination as a means by which employers weaken the bargaining power of workers, actually increasing their profits as a result. In other words, not all economists agree about the nature of discrimination and its effects. Second, we must consider the approach of the lawyer, who is guided by the provisions of the legislation and the precedents created by the courts rather than by the wider issues of women's role in the economy or in society as a whole. For those readers who are not familiar with the legislation we provide a brief outline of its contents, and show how in practice it might be expected to influence women's relative experience in the labour market. This will serve to introduce the subsequent chapter which analyses actual decisions made in the British courts.

1. What is discrimination?

'Discrimination is a phenomenon which is so pervasive in all human societies that there is no doubt at all that it exists. It is not, however, a unitary phenomenon but a complex of a number of related forms of human behaviour, and this makes it not only hard to define but frequently difficult to comprehend fully' (Kenneth Boulding).[1] As this quotation from Boulding aptly illustrates, the problems involved in trying to come to grips with the concept of discrimination are substantial. The general presumption is that those subject to discrimination will be members of a clearly identifiable minority group. This book is almost exclusively concerned with discrimination in the labour market; and in that market, with its various imperfections, it must be recognised that inequalities exist even within well-defined majority or minority occupational groups so that it is not always clear where the most appropriate comparison is to be made. The meanings attached to discrimination extend from making simple, innocent distinctions between groups to depriving people of benefits because irrelevant criteria are used.[2] If discrimination is to imply reproach then it is clear that it must involve some notion of prejudice, inequity or the use of irrelevant criteria in the differential treatment of individuals or groups in the labour market. It has to be noted that discrimination is not simply a synonym for prejudice.[3] The latter represents a desire or intention to discriminate which may be unfulfilled, whilst the former could occur by mistake in the absence of prejudice.

One major economic theory of discrimination, pioneered by Gary Becker,[4] is taste-based and founded upon the notion of personal prejudice or aversion. Thus the employer is assumed to dislike associating with members of certain groups at the workplace and is consequently prepared to pay a premium (or sacrifice profits) in order to avoid such an association. Likewise, employees may have an aversion to working alongside (or, perhaps more important, being supervised by) members of particular groups and would either be prepared to work for a lower wage if the workforce were segregated or require greater remuneration in mixed plants. This theory was primarily developed to explain racial discrimination but people working in the field have generally been prepared to assume that similar features apply to sex discrimination. But a number of notes of caution have been expressed.[5] It is not readily apparent, for example, why men should seek to work separately from women; or why, as female labour-force participation, particularly within the 25–50 year age group, has increased, men should discriminate against their own or other men's wives. Status is undoubtedly important and is perhaps more significant than simple prejudice or aversion. It also has to be recognised that women, in general, have discontinuous labour-force experience because of family responsibilities. Although changes may be discerned, advanced industrial societies have up to now divided household labour so that the female has had the prime responsibility for child care. The same considerations do not apply to different treatment between blacks and whites of

5

the same sex. Thus, whilst there are some similarities between sexual and racial discrimination, there are also some important differences.

One simple operational definition of discrimination, at least in principle, which takes into account some of these differences, defines it as the receipt of lower pay for given productivity.[6] In essence this is analogous to the concept of equal pay for work of equal value. However, it does obscure the fact that equally productive workers may receive different levels of pay for reasons other than discrimination.[7] Thus, as is obvious from casual inspection, equally productive males do not necessarily (or even usually) receive equal pay. An alternative definition proposed by the authors in an earlier work[8] is that discrimination consists of any form of unequal treatment between groups which does not directly result in cost minimisation in relation to labour utilisation, or with respect to employee discrimination which does not directly result in the maximisation of the total wage bill. Thus, in the former case, if women are cheaper (and equally productive) we would expect profit-maximising (non-discriminatory) employers to hire more women in a competitive labour market to the exclusion of men. Under these circumstances a discriminatory employer cannot be producing at minimum cost. In the latter case, one view of trade union behaviour is that union negotiators attempt to make the wage bill of the employer, and thus the income of union members, as large as possible. In theory it can be shown that if unions refuse to allow employers to take on women, when it would be cheaper for them to do so, the employer may contract output so that the total wage bill is reduced.

The above definition of discrimination is essentially designed to cover those practices which do not result in efficient outcomes. But there is a major problem with such an approach, namely the lack of information available to the employer at the time of hiring an individual. We have already noted that hiring decisions are very important in determining the employment and wage distributions, and an alleged lack of access to higher-paying, career-structured jobs is frequently a cause for concern amongst women. Let us look at the hiring decision in a little more detail to try to gain an insight into the meaning of discrimination and why the proposed definition may be inadequate.

Prior to employment, the employer does not know how successful any given individual will be at performing the tasks assigned to him or her. However, the employer is likely to have an appreciation of certain personal characteristics which seem to have been associated with good employees in the past. These characteristics may include such factors as, for example, academic attainment (C.S.E., 'O' level, 'A' level or degree qualifications), references, hobbies and interests. Certain readily observed characteristics signal something to the employer about a potential employee. Some of these characteristics, such as educational qualifications, can be acquired by individuals and indeed, to take education as an example, it is generally true that more-able individuals find it easier, and hence cheaper, to acquire these characteristics than the less able. But there are also observable characteristics that may be used by the employer in making a decision but which are not under the control of the individual, such as sex, age and race. Indeed, the employer may make assumptions about other characteristics on the basis of the group to which the individual belongs. For instance, the employer may believe, rightly or wrongly, that females are less reliable and have a higher turnover and absentee rate than males as a group. It is not possible for the employer to assess the reliability of any one worker who is being considered for a job. Thus, an individual woman who has a high potential attendance rate or level of performance may be excluded from employment on grounds which are quite rational in terms of cost minimisation, but are inequitable in terms of her own attributes. It may be thought desirable to attempt to outlaw any such behaviour by the employer based on group norms but, as Stiglitz[9] has pointed out, such an outcome would be inefficient for maximising potential output.

The above discussion has highlighted the fact that in any discussion of discrimination there are important value judgements at stake, and that there are likely to be costs, as well as benefits, involved in introducing anti-discrimination legislation. Indeed, the definition of discrimination used by the law in equal-pay and equal-opportunities legislation may differ from that which might be adopted by economists, and there is no reason to expect consistency. If the beliefs held by employers are, in fact, mistaken then the legal approach may be a step towards greater efficiency. The employers' rationalisation of decisions and determination of hiring practices will undoubtedly be based on previous experience, and if women have not been given opportunities in the more demanding jobs there will be no basis from which to infer group behaviour. It is becoming clear that there is, and will always be, a distinction between individual

7

performance and group norms. Economics is not really equipped to handle individual cases, its main strength lies in its ability to generate, and seek to refute, hypotheses about group behaviour. The statistical techniques used in such hypothesis testing are, of course, based on the laws of large numbers. However, lawyers are primarily concerned with the details of each individual case and the precise formal arguments and specific factors which lead to a particular judgement rather than any general theory involved. As Rowley has noted:[10]

> Lawyers seek out the universal 'truth' of the law by a careful selection of a number of singular statements encompassed in the judgements of the courts. For the most part, they are right to do so, since this is the thrust of precedent in the English law. But the movement from singular to universal statements is anathema to the deductive traditions which almost all economists employ.

Differences in the approaches of economists and lawyers to the existence of discrimination are examined further in Chapter 5.

Given that there are many facets to discrimination it is important to understand the sources of discrimination and the gains and losses involved. We turn to these issues in the next section.

2. Theories of discrimination

If one is to gain some understanding of the problems of measuring and tackling discrimination, it is important to comprehend the possible mechanisms at work and the motives and causes of discrimination. Accordingly, in this section we provide a brief review of the main alternative theories of discrimination that have been proposed by economists.

As noted earlier, one of the landmarks in the study of the economics of discrimination was the publication of Gary Becker's book.[11] The theory developed in that work derived from an individualistic approach where either employers or workers have a taste for discrimination. The exercise of this preference involves a cost, in terms of either the profit or the wage sacrifice the individual is prepared to suffer, which is measured by the discrimination coefficient. Becker took these tastes as given and did not seek to explain their origins. He was mainly concerned with the implications of these preferences for both individual behaviour and society. Thus,

as LaMond[12] points out: 'By defining discrimination as an exogen-
ously given "taste", neo-classical economists have merely traced the
economic consequences of discriminatory preferences. This approach
ignores the inter-relation between market outcomes and the formulation of individual attitudes, and thus adds little to our understanding of the process of ending discrimination.'

In the taste-based theories, the aversion to employing or working
with members of a minority group seems to rest on the concept of
physical distance. For example, if there is no direct contact between
the employer and certain groups of workers, why should the former
be prepared to sacrifice profits by discriminating? This consideration
has led several authors[13] to suggest that such physical-distance
models, at least of employer discrimination, are more appropriate
to white-collar than blue-collar employment since it is the former
group which is in closest contact with management. Similarly, one
might argue that relationships between managers and workers are
likely to be closer in smaller establishments which, therefore, might
be expected to exhibit greater discrimination. In addition, labour-
intensive production processes might be more prone to discrimination than those which are capital-intensive on similar grounds.[14] If
physical proximity is important, one might also expect market
discrimination to be greatest against the most highly educated
members of minority groups.

As has been mentioned before, physical distance would seem to
have little relevance to sex discrimination but in this case social
distance may be the crucial factor. Status considerations may well
be important, particularly where the issue of female supervision of
males arises. Further, family status and the division of labour within
the household are likely to play a central part in the labour-market
behaviour of women, a consideration which does not apply to
comparisons between, say, blacks and whites of the same sex. Some
of the difference in earnings between men and women is more
properly related to marital status than to discrimination. In particular, most married women face the prospect of discontinuous work
experience and some constraint on their job mobility. As emphasised
by several writers,[15] one of the principal effects of marriage on
labour-market behaviour may be to limit the job horizons of the
female partner. If both partners wish to work there is a geographic
constraint on the search for a pair of jobs. It will be rare for the
best wage offer to be produced in the same location for both husband

and wife. In most cases, therefore, there will have to be compromise (or dictatorial rule imposed). On average it will be the case that the male has greater qualifications in terms of education and training than the female and that he will work longer hours. In these circumstances, family-income maximisation would demand that the husband make a smaller concession than the wife. Such an argument leads to the prediction that, on average, married women will earn less than married men with identical personal characteristics.[16]

A second aspect of marriage is the raising of children and its effects on labour-force participation. The typical role specialisation within the family has led men to specialise in market work and women to specialise in domestic work, which includes bringing up children. As a result, as Greenhalgh notes,[17] married men tend to adopt a somewhat more ambitious attitude to work than married women as a consequence of their family roles. Further, marriage and a career tend to be complementary for men but competitive for women. Indeed, the empirical evidence suggests that the presence of children in the family is associated with higher earnings for males, but lower for females.[18] Hence differences in marital status may go some way to explaining earnings differentials and these factors should be controlled for when measuring discrimination. We use this basis in Chapter 5.

Once it is recognised that the division of labour within the family is likely to lead married women to have discontinuous labour-force participation, a number of implications for labour-market behaviour follow. These have been carefully studied by Mincer and Polachek,[19] who point out three consequences. First, where male and female earnings are compared for those who have otherwise-identical current personal characteristics, the females will have lower earnings if their past labour-market experience is shorter. Second, women will tend to undertake smaller amounts of education and training because they spend less time in market work recouping the costs involved (incidentally, this argument also provides a possible reason why an employer may be less willing to take on a female for a job involving substantial training. As noted earlier, individual women may be the victim of the general behaviour of their group). Third, the interruption of work for any period of time can cause acquired job skills to depreciate in value or atrophy. In these circumstances women will tend to choose occupations where any depreciation of skills is minimal. Such occupations are likely to be those which have lower average pay.[20]

On this last point, some recent empirical work in the United States has suggested that depreciation of skills does not occur to any great extent as a result of intermittent labour-force participation. Similarly, a study of the teaching profession in England[21] has shown that both men and women who returned to teaching after a break of two years or more suffered no loss of earnings when compared to other teachers with a similar length of completed service. In this latter case, however, it is not clear whether the result is simply a function of the particular salary structure or whether intermittent labour-force participation really is unimportant. The crucial factor for the returning woman is whether an incremental pay structure is related to age or experience.

A further important question is the impact on earnings of the frequency and timing of absences from the labour force. In general, men withdraw from the labour force for relatively short spells, frequently at the start of their careers and for reasons which often involve the acquisition of further skills through education and training. Women, on the other hand, tend to have longer spells of withdrawal which are spread out over the working life and which rarely involve skill acquisition.[22]

Whilst the size of any depreciation of skills as a result of intermittent labour-force participation is open to question it seems pretty clear that the fact and expectation of intermittent participation on the part of women does influence the amount of training undertaken. Duncan and Hoffman,[23] for example, find that in the United States past interruptions to work experience did lead to significantly lower amounts of training for black women; past part-time work had the same effect for white women; and the expectation of children similarly reduced the likelihood that women of both races would undertake training.

For all the above reasons, it is important to take cognisance of the traditional female role within the family in any analysis of discrimination. It does not follow, however, that all of the male–female wage differential is explicable in terms of factors deriving from the family role of women; discrimination could still play a major role.

If discrimination arises from tastes and preferences of employers and workers, and they are individualistic, as the Becker analysis presumes, it follows that there will be significant differences in the magnitude of any aversion to employing or working with women on the part of males. To take the case of employer discrimination, those with the least dislike of female employees will have the lowest costs. It would be expected, therefore, that over time non-discriminators would be able to expand at the expense of discriminators and that discrimination would eventually be removed by this competitive process. The implication of the Becker model is that discrimination in only likely to prevail where the possibility of competition is relatively remote. Attempts to test this hypothesis in private industry by controlling for the amount of market power, and in the government sector – which might be argued to be divorced from competitive pressures – have met with mixed results.[24] Statistical measurement of market power is, however, notoriously difficult and the available measures are necessarily crude[25] so that such a result is perhaps not surprising.

One implication sometimes drawn from the Becker analysis is that discrimination cannot exist since it is incompatible with profit maximisation under competitive conditions; but such a conclusion is unwarranted, as perfect competition, with perfect information, is not the norm in most, if not all, markets. It remains plausible, however, despite our inability to measure it, that there is some link between imperfections of competition and discrimination. But once managers have some discretion because of the reduction of competitive forces, they can exercise this in various ways. It does not follow, however, that they will choose to exercise this discretion through discrimination since there may be more attractive alternatives.

One other important contribution of Becker's was to analyse the distribution of the costs and benefits of discrimination. If, for example, it could be shown that those who discriminate gain in a monetary sense from their actions, there would be no need to look any further for an explanation of their behaviour and no necessity to have recourse to tastes, aversion or prejudice. According to Becker, however, not only is national income reduced by discrimination, but both groups, the majority and the minority, are worse off as a consequence. But it has been argued that such a conclusion rests heavily on the presumption of individualistic behaviour in the Becker model. If the majority operate as a group it is possible for them to gain at the expense of the minority.[26] This leads on naturally to the suggestion that bargaining or monopoly power models of discrimination are more appropriate than those based on individual behaviour. As Boulding notes,[27] monopoly power in the labour market may be exercised in a number of ways including occupational licensing, trade union restrictions on entry or informal hiring practices, but its main purpose is to obtain job control and higher incomes.

An alternative but related approach is that of dual-labour-market theory, which views prime-age (white) males as being concentrated in high-paid, stable jobs which offer training, promotion and career prospects – the so-called primary jobs, whereas most women (and black workers) are trapped in low-paid, insecure secondary jobs which offer no prospects of advancement. The problem is increased to the extent that confinement to secondary jobs affects the motivation of workers and their job performance, time-keeping and attendance. For females, the argument is frequently expressed in terms of the crowding hypothesis,[28] where lack of access to male-dominated jobs causes them to be overcrowded into a relatively small range of occupations and that this abundance of supply has a further depressing effect on wages. If this crowding has resulted from male domination, the operation of equal-opportunities legislation could have a substantial impact on the relative position of women. If occupations were opened up to women, not only would there be improvements in their absolute wage rates but there would be changes in relative wage rates. Thus, the male-dominated occupations would suffer a relative decline in earnings as competition from females increased, whereas those in female-dominated occupations would rise. The clear corollary is that male incomes would fall. But the removal of the depressing effect of crowding on female productivity would tend to lead to a more efficient allocation of labour and a rise in national income. The net effects of all these changes are difficult to quantify and there remains the problem of the extent to which the preponderance of women in some occupations is a direct result of discrimination by males. As we have noted, there are many reasons why male and female occupational and earnings distributions would be unequal even in the absence of any discrimination. Although the crowding hypothesis may help to explain some of the difference in earnings between men and women, it does not really bring us any nearer to an understanding of the concept of discrimination.

Finally, mention should be made of the views of radical economists on the nature of discrimination. Radical economists hold that capitalists deliberately segment labour markets in order to divide workers so that they do not form a cohesive group to challenge management. According to one recent model,[29] such a divide-and-conquer strategy will force down the wages of both white and black workers. Further, employers will deliberately integrate their workforces in order to prevent unity among the workers and reduce the probability of strike action. At the same time employee discrimination results in a wage differential in mixed workforces. Thus, in contrast to Becker's model, discrimination is a function of the profit-maximising behaviour of the employer, together with non-wage-bill maximising on the part of workers. Again this theory was largely developed in relation to racial discrimination and it is not readily apparent why a policy of sexual integration should necessarily reduce the cohesion of the workers, unless unionism is reduced through the influx of women and this in turn weakens the bargaining power of the union. Further, as noted in the following chapter, there is no evidence that male–female wage differentials are systematically lower in capitalist countries *vis-a-vis* socialist countries, though the relationship between discrimination and political structures has not been investigated.

In this section we have presented a brief review of the major theories that have been put forward to explain persistent differences in the earnings of men and women. We have argued that the issue of sex discrimination is more complicated than that of race because the division of labour within the household has a profound effect on the labour-market behaviour of women. It seems to us that just as there are no simple diagnoses so there can be no simple cure. It is with this in mind that we turn to an examination of the legal framework in the u.k.

3. Equal-pay and equal-opportunities legislation in Britain

Detailed comments on the interpretation of the law by tribunals and courts are contained in Chapter 4. In this section we seek merely to set out the main points of the two relevant Acts. It might be argued that these are sufficiently well known to make the present section superfluous but, as we show in Chapter 4, there is still widespread ignorance of the terms of the legislation amongst the affected parties. Nevertheless, those readers who are aware of the broad terms of the legislation are advised to proceed to the next section.

Economic and legal perspectives

The Equal Pay Act was passed in 1970 and, following a transition period, came into full force at the end of 1975. The Act is designed to prevent inequalities in the terms and conditions of employment between men and women, but it does not seek to ensure equality of opportunity of access to jobs. Such a task was assigned to the Sex Discrimination Act which was passed in 1975. The objective of the Equal Pay Act is to be achieved in two main ways. First, men and women are to be paid the same if they are employed on the same or broadly similar work. For the job to qualify as 'broadly similar', the differences between the things men do and the things women do should not be of practical importance – in frequency as well as nature. Such a clause does involve fine problems of interpretation, and the subsequent case law on this point is examined in Chapter 4. The provision was widened somewhat to cover equal pay for different jobs which have been rated as equivalent under a job-evaluation exercise. Second, the Central Arbitration Committee,[30] when called upon, was empowered to remove discrimination in collective agreements, employers' pay structures and statutory wage orders which contain provisions applying specifically to men only or women only. Agreements or pay structures can also be referred to the committee so that rates applying specifically to women can be brought up to the lowest male rate in the agreement or pay structure. This was broadly achieved by 1976.

Unequal treatment between a man and a woman can be justified if the employer can prove that any difference between the two contracts is due to a material difference (other than that of gender). The terms of the Act apply to male and female workers employed by the same employer, or associated employer, at the same establishment, or establishments, in Great Britain, at which common terms and conditions of employment are observed either generally or for employees of the relevant classes.

In the field of employment, the Sex Discrimination Act prohibits discrimination with respect to hiring, opportunities for promotion, transfer and training, and dismissal procedures on grounds of gender or marriage. Thus it should be noted that the Act offers protection to married persons of either sex, to single men and women separately, but not to single persons as a group. The discrimination provisions relate to two forms of discrimination – direct and indirect. The former arises, for example, where a woman is treated, because she is female, less favourably than a man would be treated in circumstances which

15

are the same or not materially different. The latter occurs where a requirement or condition is applied to a woman which is applied or would apply to a man but: (i) which is such that the proportion of women who can comply with it is considerably smaller than the proportion of men who can comply with it; (ii) which the employer cannot show to be justifiable irrespective of the sex of the person to whom it is applied; (iii) which is to her detriment because she cannot comply with it.

The coverage of such indirect discrimination mirrors developments in the United States and is an important aspect of the law which raises substantial practical and conceptual problems. It also appears to be an area of the legislation over which there is much confusion and, again, we develop the discussion in Chapter 4.

The Act applies equally to men and women and it follows that reverse discrimination (i.e. that in favour of women) is generally unlawful. Thus, the legislation does not involve any affirmative action proposals of the type used in the United States. The one exception is that the Act permits special access to training facilities for one sex only, where, within the previous twelve months, there were no persons of the sex in question performing that work or the numbers so doing were comparatively small.

As with the Equal Pay Act, an individual has the right to take his or her case to an industrial tribunal. In the event of an action being brought under the Sex Discrimination Act, the burden of proof is upon the complainant to show the existence of a particular requirement and that it operated to his or her detriment. If this case is accepted, the burden of proof transfers to the employer to demonstrate that the requirement is justified. The Equal Opportunities Commission, established under the Act, has the power, amongst others, to carry out formal investigations into organisations and to issue non-discrimination notices. Given this provision of the law, it is imperative that employers should have available detailed analyses of the type outlined in this book.

4. The impact of legal intervention on equal pay and equal opportunities for women

We discuss in the next chapter the main features of the overall picture of male–female wage differentials in Britain. But, as pointed out earlier, the main thrust of the legislation is directed towards the position of women within particular establishments, and it is appropriate in this section, first, to review the evidence as to what has happened at the level of the organisation and, second, to offer some suggestions as to the likely significance of such legislation in the light of our theoretical discussions.

On the first of these points, we can do no better than to quote from recently published research findings on the implementation and effects of the Equal Pay and Sex Discrimination Acts in 26 organisations.[31] After lengthy and detailed study the authors of the report conclude:

> Women have made tangible gains as a result of the Acts, particularly with respect to pay. The vast majority of women in the organisations studied were entitled to and received some increase in their rates of pay as a result of the Equal Pay Act and most were getting equal pay as defined by the Act. As a result of the Sex Discrimination Act, most overt forms of discrimination in employment had disappeared and some job opportunities were opened to women which formerly were closed to them. But while the legislation can be deemed largely successful in this rather narrow sense, it cannot be said to have had much success in achieving equal pay and opportunities in the wider sense.

The authors identify a number of problem areas which they argue account for the limited success of the legislation, and they may be listed as follows:

(i) a large number of women are not, in practice, covered by the Equal Pay Act because there are no men with whom they can be compared on a 'like work' basis;

(ii) the considerable lawful underpayment of women because of strategies by employers to reduce the scope of the comparisons between men and women under the Act;

(iii) the number of either clear-cut or potential cases of non-compliance with the Act which women either failed to identify or failed to act upon;

(iv) women continued to receive lower pay than men, even where the Act was complied with, since they were generally in the lower-graded jobs and in lower-paid industries;

(v)   continuing job segregation despite the Sex Discrimination Act;
(vi) the number of cases of direct or indirect discrimination which
      would have been unlawful under the Sex Discrimination Act but
      which were not recognised or acted upon by either the women
      themselves or the unions.

They end with the conclusion that little further progress is likely
in the workplace without some further intervention to stimulate
action.

There are two main strands here in explaining the limited success
of equal-opportunities legislation. First, there is the fact that the
legislation has been under-utilised, perhaps because of ignorance.
Second, there is the fact that its scope is limited. The latter partly
reflects the substantial differences on the supply side between men
and women which we have already highlighted. As Ivy Papps argues,
there is a fundamental problem with the definition of equal work
under the Equal Pay Act:[32] 'That two workers are doing the same
job is no guarantee that they are doing the same work. They may
have different productivity.'

She suggests that differential productivity will arise from differences in physical strength (though as we note later this is likely to be
of declining significance), from higher absenteeism because women
continue to accept the primary responsibility for their families, and
from the fact that maternity-leave provisions in the legislation make
women more expensive than men. The enforcement of equal pay,
despite differences in productivity and costs, will harm women who
are not considered by employers to be cost-efficient at the higher
wages, and who become unemployed as a consequence. The Sex
Discrimination Act compounds the problem, since to some extent
it prevents employers from reducing their relative demand for women.
But, in the long run, employers will have an incentive to substitute
capital for labour, or they may be forced out of business. Papps
concludes that there are no indications that the Equal Pay Act will
help women as a whole. Other legislation, such as the Employment
Protection Act which, amongst other provisions, includes paid
maternity rights which help women to return to work, may further
increase the pressure on employers to prefer males on grounds of cost.

It is certainly worth emphasising that the legislation is not likely
to have any dramatic effect on male–female relative earnings overall.
We have argued that there are many reasons why the male and

female earnings and occupational structures are not equal; and women as a whole have been restricted by the traditional division of labour in the family which assigns them to periods of intermittent labour-force participation through family circumstances. It is clear, from both theory and practice, that factors such as education, experience and training are important determinants of earnings and, as we shall see in Chapters 3 and 5, a high proportion of the male–female earnings differential can be explained by these factors. Equal-pay and equal-opportunities legislation will have important feedback effects on the acquisition of these personal characteristics which provide some form of signal to the employer as to the worth of the individual. Career prospects and incentives may be opened to women as the result of legislation, but whether there is any marked change in the relative position of women over the long run will to a large extent be dependent upon what happens within or to the family unit.

That one should not expect too much from legislation is illustrated by the experience in the United States under the affirmative action programme where those receiving Federal contracts were to correct deficiencies in their employment of minorities and women, failure to do so possibly leading to loss of any such contracts. A number of careful studies of the effects of this policy have been undertaken and the results are well summarised by Ashenfelter:[33]

> Together these studies suggest that, as a result of the contract compliance program, minority employment in firms with government contracts has been significantly increased relative to what otherwise would have been the case. The results are quantitatively small, however, and certainly do not establish the presumption that this government programme has been the major force behind the growth in the relative earnings of black workers.

Ashenfelter's conclusions relate to race and, as we have already noted, there may be significant differences between racial and sexual discrimination. Interestingly, two papers presented at a recent conference on women in the labour market, held in New York, have suggested a somewhat more favourable impact of anti-discrimination legislation on the male–female wage differential in the United State.[34] Andrea Beller reports that the male–female wage differential remained virtually constant between 1967 and 1974 despite the

19

existence of Title VII of the Civil Rights Act of 1964, the Equal Employment Opportunity Title, and its amendment in 1972. But she argues that this represents an improvement in the position of women since their rising labour-force participation over the period would have been expected to increase the differential. This increase would have come about since the new female entrants to the labour force would have less labour-market experience than existing members and hence command lower wages. Without Title VII, she argues, the male–female earnings differential would have widened by about seven percentage points. Edward Lazear argues that use of the current wage or earnings differential is a misleading indicator of progress since what really matters is the growth of income over the working life of the individual. In the past, male incomes have tended to grow rather faster than female incomes over the individual's lifetime because of the greater investment in training by men. Taking young workers, he demonstrates a substantial narrowing of the male–female wage differential between 1968 and 1974. In particular, he argues that the rise in the relative earnings of young females arose from an increase in their rate of wage growth, which reflects their increased investment in on-the-job training. Thus, he concludes that the profile of female earnings over the working life will diverge from that of males to a much smaller extent than it did in the past.

The three conference discussants[35] of these two papers did, however, point out a number of conceptual and data limitations of the analyses and said that the statistical significance of the findings was rather weak. It seems appropriate, therefore, to retain an open mind on the quantitative magnitude of any changes in relative female earnings as a result of anti-discrimination legislation. It is worth noting, however, that even the most favourable studies still leave a substantial gap between male and female earnings; and it should not be expected that the enforcement of equal-pay and equal-opportunities laws will produce anything like equality in the male and female earnings distributions.

It also needs to be recognised that most of the studies of the impact of legislation were conducted using data prior to the impact of the recession which occurred in the late 1970s in many advanced countries, including in particular the U.K. and the U.S.A. As unemployment in Britain reaches 3 million and as school leavers of both sexes find it increasingly difficult to obtain a job one wonders whether there is much scope for an improvement in the relative position of women over the short or medium term. In addition, clerical and administrative jobs, which currently use large numbers of women, are perhaps those most at risk from advances in micro-technology.

In the chapters that follow we seek to amplify and build upon the points made in this introduction, and we pay particular attention to ways in which organisations can assess their own treatment of females, the importance of controlling for differences in productivity and the extent to which they are complying with the spirit, if not necessarily the letter, of the law.

3
The male–female earnings differential in Britain[1]

1. Introduction

The evidence available suggests conclusively that average earnings for women are well below those of men in virtually every country where statistics on earnings classified by sex are published; although one has to be cautious about comparing earnings distributions in different countries, particularly as far as Eastern Europe is concerned.[2] Women's relative earnings are lower in the English-speaking countries but it does not appear that there is much difference between variants of capitalist and socialist economic systems. Thus, in countries such as the U.S., the U.K., Canada and Australia women have tended to earn on average less than 60 per cent of male average earnings, whilst in such diverse countries as Czechoslovakia, Finland, France, Hungary, Israel, Norway and Poland the figure lies between 65 and 70 per cent. Further, fragmentary evidence suggests that the picture is not vastly different in the Soviet Union, China and Cuba. Lower pay for women is, therefore, a universal phenomenon and does not appear to be a function of the type of economic or social system.

Not only do gross male–female earnings appear to vary greatly between countries as outlined above, but they also appear to vary between sectors within the same country (Britain being something of an exception in the latter respect). Indeed, according to a recent United Nations study,[3] Britain is among the most unequal of the Western industrial countries with respect to female earnings as a proportion of male earnings; the figure of 50 per cent in the non-industrial sector contrasting with that of 80–87 per cent among non-industrial sectors in the country with the lowest differential – Sweden. Britain's relatively unfavourable position is also reflected in Table 3.1 which distinguishes between manual and non-manual workers. The United Nations study also points out that

Male–female earnings differential

Table 3.1: *Women's monthly earnings as a percentage of men's earnings in industry for selected European countries*

Country and Year		Manual	Non-manual
Belgium	1974–7	68.0	64.2
France	1973–7	74.6	62.0
W. Germany	1977	66.2	64.5
Italy	1974–6	82.1	68.3
Netherlands	1974–7	69.6	58.2
Sweden	1976	86.0	71.9
United States	1976	58.2	63.1
United Kingdom	1977	60.7	54.6

Source: United Nations, *The Economic Role of Women in the ECE Region*, New York, 1980.

in most countries for which data are available the average gender wage differential narrowed significantly during the 1970s, the change in Britain being amongst the largest. Despite this there is no direct evidence that the rising pay of women relative to men has resulted, as one might expect, in diminishing employment opportunities for women relative to men, though any such effect may have been concealed by the growth of sectors (such as services) which currently employ a large number of women.

Within Britain, and as a rough approximation, women have earned only two-thirds as much as men for as long as wage records have been maintained. Recent figures from the New Earnings Survey suggest, however, that in Britain the relative position of women has improved, and by a substantial amount, viewed in the light of historical experience (see Table 3.2). This improvement was con-temporaneous with the implementation of equal-pay and equal-opportunities legislation, so that such a change might be attributed to this particular form of government intervention. Yet, it must be borne in mind that the 1970s included periods when wage restraint was practised in the form of (partial) flat-rate wage increases, which, because women earn less than men, have a disproportionate effect on the earnings of the former.[4] The relaxation of incomes policy guidelines might explain the deterioration in the position of women relative to men in 1978 and 1979.

Equality of opportunity would only imply equality of earnings

Tackling discrimination

Table 3.2: *Average gross hourly earnings, excluding overtime, of full-time employees aged 18 and over whose pay was not affected by absence: women as a percentage of men*

1970	63.1	1977	75.5
1974	67.4	1978	73.9
1975	72.1	1979	73.0
1976	75.1	1980	73.5

Source: New Earnings Survey results reported in the Employment Gazette, Vol. 88, No. 10, October 1980.

Note: The figures are not comparable with those of Table 3.1 as they exclude overtime and relate to all workers (manual and non-manual) in all sectors (not just industry)

for men and women if the two groups were identical with respect to those attributes which attract a price in the market. Even if we accept that women are discriminated against in the labour market, removal of discrimination will only close the male–female earnings gap to the extent that discrimination is a major component of it. As the British Employment Gazette notes, 'comparisons of men's and women's earnings reflect not only the level of earnings but also the different employment patterns and other labour-force characteristics. From a survey like the N.E.S. [New Earnings Survey] it is not possible to comment on relative earnings on a "for equal work" basis. However, the detailed volumes of survey results enable the effects of the main differences in the structures of men's and women's employment on earnings to be assessed.'[5] It is necessary then to consider factors which might contribute to this earnings gap. These include: (i) education and training which lead to differences in occupational distributions, (ii) marriage, which means that many women have discontinuous labour-market service and less experience than men, (iii) differences in motivation, performance and working hours and (iv) variations in the extent of union organisation.

2. Education and training

The level of education received prior to entry into the labour market and the amount and nature of on- or off-the-job training received thereafter have an appreciable effect on earnings. As the Equal Opportunities Commission[6] has pointed out, traditional specialisation in schools strongly influences choice of subject, with boys tending towards scientific subjects and girls towards art subjects. Thus nearly five times as many boys as girls obtain 'A' level passes in physics and substantial differences apply in other disciplines. Further, whilst levels of educational attainment are only marginally different between the sexes, many more boys than girls join degree courses, so that, according to 1976 figures, only slightly more than one-third of university first-degree graduates are women. As later reflected in employment, these female graduates tend to be concentrated in particular disciplines – over 60 per cent of undergraduates in literature or languages, but less than 5 per cent in engineering or technological subjects.[7] Women graduates are much more likely than men to enter public service or education and much less likely to enter industry and commerce. There are a number of factors which might explain these sex differences in level and type of educational attainment. For instance, it is possible that cultural traditions and differences in tastes influence skill acquisition or that expected future family commitments or expectations of market discrimination reduce women's demand for education in particular subjects. Whatever the reason, there is no doubting the importance of educational level on future earnings potential. This is revealed in rate-of-return estimates which attempt to measure the direct monetary benefits of education. These are calculated as the earnings differential of the qualified over the unqualified during the working lifetime, and are discounted by the market rate of interest to allow for the fact that income received in the future is valued less than income received now. There is, in fact, no clear evidence that the rate of return on education in Britain is lower for women than for men, but it remains true that women's earnings are appreciably lower than those of men at the same level of educational qualification. However, the male–female differential varies inversely with educational level. This might be explained by the comparative advantage of men in jobs requiring physical strength. On the other hand both sexes are equally endowed with intelligence and this becomes progressively more important than physical strength as jobs increase in skill and complexity.

In addition to education, an important influence on earnings is the provision by employers of possibilities for training and retraining whilst in employment. Employers will realise, however, that the payback period from any investment in training will be shorter in the case of women whose turnover rates are generally significantly higher than they are for men. Consequently, employers may be reluctant to provide either on- or off-the-job training for women. Thus, Department of Education and Science statistics reveal that in 1976 only 96,000 women, compared to 436,000 men, were enrolled on part-time day-release courses in major further education establishments in England and Wales. The question of retraining is particularly important for those women who wish to re-enter the labour market after a period of absence engaged on family or household duties.

3. Occupational differences

Many authors have pointed to the differences in employment patterns between the sexes. In Britain over two-thirds of women are employed in non-manual occupations compared with not much more than one-third of men, and no less than 40 per cent of all employed women are in clerical occupations and a further 20 per cent (approximately) in occupations related to education, health and welfare. This kind of occupational division can be referred to as horizontal occupational segregation, but we must also allow for vertical occupational segregation – the fact that within occupational groups men tend to predominate in the higher grades. In the former case Hakim[8] finds conflicting trends for Britain over the period 1901 to 1971. Whilst the proportion of occupations which were wholly male fell to 2 per cent in 1971 (after being relatively constant at 9 per cent over the period 1901–61), the proportion of occupations in which women were greatly over-represented (taken to be 70 per cent or more of the workforce) actually increased slightly from 9 per cent to 12 per cent. As for vertical occupational segregation, Hakim finds that the proportion of women in managerial, administrative, lower-professional and technical occupations fell between 1911 and 1961 (recovering somewhat by 1971), whilst in manual work the trend is unambiguously towards greater segregation, with men being increasingly over-represented in skilled jobs and women in semi- and unskilled jobs. These differences in occupational distributions are naturally enough reflected in differences in pay.[9] An earlier study by the authors[10] suggests, however, that differences in pay within broad occupational groups contribute much more to the gross earnings differential between the sexes than does the different distribution of the sexes among the various occupations. That is, if one hypothetically paid women the average male earnings in their existing occupations, this would raise female average earnings overall by much more than if women were hypothetically redistributed by occupation so that their occupational distribution accorded with that of men. To some extent this may reflect the importance of incremental payment systems in non-manual occupations where the majority of women are found. Since women on average have fewer years' experience than men in particular occupations, they will earn less than men where wage scales tie earnings to length of service. Also important is the fact that for many married women job choices are constrained by the location of their husband's job and by restrictions on their ability to accept jobs far from home on account of family responsibilities and lack of easy access to transport facilities. There are more small establishments than large, so there is a greater probability of finding a small employer close to home than a large employer. As a consequence, women are more likely than men to be found in small establishments which tend on average to pay less. Neither of these factors is likely to be much influenced by equality-of-opportunities legislation, since this does not as a general rule disallow extra payment for additional seniority, nor seek to impose equality of pay for given occupations across (as opposed to within) firms.

4. Marital status

As pointed out in Chapter 2 the British Sex Discrimination Act 1975 makes it unlawful to discriminate against a worker in terms of job recruitment, promotion or dismissal because he or she is married. Married women have increased their participation in the labour force substantially. In Great Britain in 1911 only 9.6 per cent of married women were in the labour force, by 1951 the figure was still only 21.7 per cent yet by 1979 this had risen to 51.3 per cent. Department of Employment estimates suggest that by 1991 married women will constitute no less than 28.7 per cent of the entire labour force. It is, therefore, important to take into account the possible effects of marital status on the male–female earnings differential.

As we discussed in Chapter 2, marriage is likely to have a number of effects on the labour-market behaviour of women. In the first place it may tend to limit their job horizons since the family may give first priority to the selection of a suitable job for the husband. Second, the raising of children has a marked impact on labour-force participation and both the number and ages of children are likely to influence the decision whether or not to work and, if so, the number of hours to work. Empirical studies reveal that the presence of children does have a depressing effect on female earnings.[11] We also discussed the consequences which arise from the discontinuous labour-market experience and the corresponding breaks in service.[12] The implication of these factors is that we would expect married women to earn less than single women or men, other things being equal. Unfortunately many earnings data do not differentiate between workers on the basis of marital status to allow firm estimates to be made of the extent to which this depresses female earnings overall.

In contrast to the above, some studies have found that marriage has a positive effect on the earnings of men, when other factors such as age are held constant. This might be a consequence of (i) married men being more work-motivated than single men because of their additional family responsibilities, (ii) paternalistic attitudes on the part of employers which lead them to reward those with greater financial responsibilities with higher earnings or, possibly, (iii) because men who are personally more acceptable both get married and perform better in jobs. In order to isolate sex discrimination, therefore, it seems safer to limit the comparison to single men and single women for whom attitudes to work and career orientation might be held to be closest, as in the studies by Greenhalgh[13] and Siebert and Sloane[14] which will be discussed in Chapter 5.

5. Age and experience

In many jobs pay is age- or experience-related. In part this reflects the fact that certain skills are specific to particular employers and competence in them increases with experience. It is possible to construct age–earnings or experience–earnings profiles which

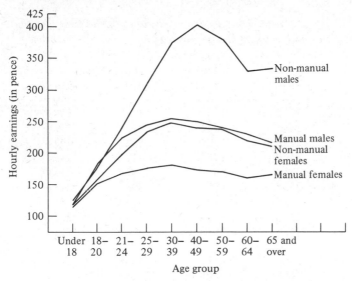

Figure 3.1 Average gross hourly earnings by age, April 1980 (in pence).
Source: New Earnings Survey

bring out this relationship, as in Figure 3.1 drawn from the results of the 1980 New Earnings Survey. This shows that, at each age, males in non-manual work earn more than those in manual work, who in turn earn slightly more on average than females in non-manual work, with females in manual work earning least of all.[15] As shown in Table 3.3 female earnings in manual and non-manual work peak in the 30–39 age group (when a substantial number of women are out of the labour force)[16] though the peak for men in non-manual work is reached later in the 40–49 age group. It can be seen that an important contributory factor towards the lower earnings of women overall is that age–earnings profiles are flatter than those for men, or, in other words, the rate of return to age or experience is less for women than for men. It is not clear whether the reason for this is the reluctance of women to undertake further training or the failure of employers to offer such opportunities.

6. Productivity and related factors

As noted in the section on education and training it is not safe to assume that the various sex/marital status groups are equally

29

Table 3.3: *Average gross hourly earnings by age, April 1980 (in pence): ful-time males and females whose pay was not affected by absence*

Age	Manual males	Manual females	Non-manual males	Non-manual females
Under 18	117.2	115.6	122.0	118.6
18–20	183.3	152.0	178.6	159.0
21–24	225.0	170.0	243.8	199.4
25–29	247.7	178.3	311.3	236.4
30–39	255.3	181.9	377.5	250.0
40–49	252.8	175.4	408.3	243.3
50–59	241.9	172.9	384.3	240.3
60–64	232.2	163.2	333.1	224.4
65 and over	219.5	167.1	336.5	214.1
18 and over	241.4	172.1	351.8	221.2
21 and over	245.8	174.8	360.8	232.5
All ages	237.3	168.8	348.1	216.2

motivated or as capable with respect to work performance on various tasks. In 1919 the Atkin Committee, basing its judgement on piece-rate earnings data, commented that as a general rule women were capable of producing only four-fifths of a man's average output on manual work, but technological change has undoubtedly rendered this estimate suspect under modern conditions. There are in fact surprisingly few studies which have attempted to compare the output of men and women under comparable circumstances, though such studies that have been undertaken, for instance in academic work, suggest we cannot rule out the importance of such differences.[17] Perhaps more significant, however, are sex differences in absenteeism and the rate at which men and women voluntarily leave firms (quit rates). These are noticeably higher for women, at least in younger age groups, even when allowance is made for the different occupational distributions of the sexes, but estimates of the costs imposed on employers suggest that such differences can only explain a small proportion of the overall male–female earnings differential. It is possible, too, that managers exaggerate the size and significance of such differences.

7. The components of pay

Men and women differ in the extent to which their pay is influenced by overtime,[18] shift-working and payment-by-results. Overtime and shift-work attract premium rates of pay. Similarly, where variations in effort or performance are directly rewarded by additional payment there may be considerable variations in the level of earnings, even in the same occupation. For instance, New Earnings Survey data suggest that in 1980 these three components of pay contributed 26.1 per cent of weekly earnings for men compared with 14.5 per cent for women in manual occupations, and 6.7 per cent for men compared with only 3.2 per cent for women in non-manual occupations. This reflects both the greater size of such payments to men and the fact that a larger proportion of men receive them. For instance, in 1980 the proportions of both sexes in receipt of overtime payments in manual and non-manual occupations respectively were 54.3 per cent and 19.6 per cent for men, and 12.9 per cent and 10.7 per cent for women. These differences would be held to be discriminatory only if women who wished, for example, to work longer hours or do shift-work, were denied the opportunity to do so. Married women with household duties, in particular, may find neither of the two options attractive. We must remember, too, that women's hours of work are restricted by the Factories Act.

8. The extent of trade union organisation

Trade unions have the effect of raising the pay of their members relative to those of non-union workers through collective bargaining, or through the fact that limited employment opportunities in the unionised sector drive more workers into the non-unionised sector, thereby depressing pay in that sector. Unions could in theory either narrow the male–female earnings differential by obtaining a higher mark-up for women than for men (perhaps by reducing or even eliminating discrimination) or widen it by excluding women disproportionately to men from the benefits of unionisation. Historically a smaller proportion of the female labour force than the male have been union members, but recently women have joined trade unions at a faster rate than men. For example in 1967 only 27.2 per cent of potential female employees were union members, compared to 53.0 per cent of males, but by 1978 the figures were 38.2 per cent (a 65.7 per cent increase in absolute terms) and 60.7 per cent (a.10.4 per cent increase) respectively.[19] In the latter year 77.1 per cent of men in manual occupations were covered by some form of collective agreement compared with 70.4 per cent of women. Yet for non-manual workers coverage was greater for women (66.2 per cent) compared to men (58.0 per cent). It is the higher proportion of men in the manual groups that gives the male workforce as a whole the greater collective bargaining coverage.[20] One study, using collective bargaining coverage data, found that in 1972 the union wage effect was slightly greater for women than for men (19 per cent as opposed to 18 per cent).[21] The small difference here, allied to the large differences between the sexes in union membership, would suggest the net effect of unions in Britain has been to widen the gross male–female earnings differential. On the other hand, it appears that increasing union membership of women is likely to narrow it.

Conclusion

Equality of opportunity does not imply that men and women should on average receive the same amount of pay. It simply means paying the same wage rates to equally productive men and women. As we have seen, there are a large number of factors on both the supply and the demand sides of the labour market, of which discrimination is only one, to explain the sizeable difference found between the average earnings of men and women in Britain. Generally, the average woman coming onto the labour market has different endowments of education and skill from her male counterpart, whether as a consequence of differing preferences, fashioned by expectations of family commitments, or as a consequence of anticipated discrimination in possible future jobs. Once married they tend to leave the labour force and, on return, search for a new job in a relatively restricted area. In turn these factors make many women less attractive to particular employers, a fact which in the past led some employers to recruit women to certain occupations at lower rates of pay than men or to exclude them from these occupations altogether. The elimination of the gross net earnings differential would require men and women to be identical in terms of both tastes and value to employers in the market. That in turn would imply a revolution in family life with an equal division of household duties between men and women.

4

Monitoring discrimination and the law

Many of the clauses in the Equal Pay and Sex Discrimination Acts are imprecise. For instance, what constitutes a material difference, or what factors are likely to be construed as amounting to indirect discrimination? The impact of the legislation very much depends on how such aspects are interpreted by the courts. Therefore, it is necessary in this chapter to examine the more significant legal cases so far, in order to see how personnel practices might need to adjust to these relatively new circumstances. For firms of any size, an *ad hoc* approach is likely to be inefficient, if for no other reason than it is time-consuming to be continually adjusting procedures in the light of the most recent law case. It seems preferable to adopt an explicit equal-opportunities policy which attempts to anticipate, in a general way, which particular procedures are likely to be broadly acceptable in the light of legal developments. Therefore, we trace out the elements of an equal-opportunities policy and discuss the nature and extent of the statistics that must be maintained to make such a policy operational. In particular, we focus upon the relationship which exists between the personal characteristics of individuals and their earnings or position within the organisation. These characteristics relate to factors which are believed to affect the productivity of the individual, and attention is devoted to the question whether there appears to be any difference in the treatment of these characteristics according to whether the individual is male or female. This approach can be termed the 'earnings function' method and we explain its rationale and illustrate its application in further detail in Chapter 5.

Tackling discrimination

1. Background to the development of an equal-opportunities policy at the company level

In its investigation the Equal Opportunities Commission (E.O.C.) has found a 'massive ignorance' amongst employers of the details of the Equal Pay Act (E.P.A.) and the Sex Discrimination Act (S.D.A.) particularly in respect of the concept of indirect discrimination.[1] Such ignorance in turn reflects the fact that equality of opportunity has in general been afforded a low priority by employers partly as a consequence of difficult market conditions and partly through the fact that the two Acts were only part of what was regarded as 'an excessive and growing burden of legislation'[2], but perhaps also because many employers inclined to the view, whether erroneous or not, that inequality of opportunity was not a serious problem in their own enterprise.

The E.O.C. has stressed the importance of all relevant parties, including government departments, nationalised industries, local authorities, professional organisations, other employers and trade unions, playing a *positive* role in implementation of equality of opportunity[3] rather than merely ensuring compliance with the law. This is reflected in its recently published draft Code of Practice on Equal Employment Opportunities.[4] Yet in its survey of 500 leading employers the Commission found that only 25 per cent of respondents had written equal-opportunity policies, only 14 per cent had established executive responsibility for implementation and only 12 per cent had introduced particular policies for women.[5] The Commission has argued that there are sound economic reasons for adopting a positive approach to the matter: 'It is good business practice, apart from questions of law and justice, to assist and encourage all employees to develop their economic and individual potential. Proper selection, training and development of both female and male employees will improve their performance and strengthen their commitment, from which employers as well as employees will gain.'[6]

Though this statement does not necessarily imply that the E.O.C. is advocating an equal distribution of men and women across all occupations, it should be qualified. Given, for example, higher rates of turnover and absenteeism amongst women than men and the possibilities of different levels of performance in particular jobs for which there is some evidence,[7] it will rarely be optimal for the employer to ensure that women are equally distributed with men among all occupational groups.[8] Human capital theory[9] regards the acquisition of skill as an investment decision made in anticipation of future returns (or higher levels of earnings as a reward for skill) and thus suggests that on average it will be less profitable for a firm to invest in the training of women because the pay-back period will be shorter than that for a man. Likewise, the same will be true for a woman if it is a question of her bearing the cost of training. According to the current legislation, judgements must be made, however, on the basis of the attributes of the individual rather than on the basis of those of the group of which he or she is a member. In other words an employer cannot lawfully reject a female applicant on the basis that women tend to have higher turnover rates and absence than men. What is relevant is whether the particular woman is likely to be more prone to absence or to leave than is the case for other applicants for the job. Notwithstanding this, the cost-minimising employer would require accurate information on the relative turnover rates of men and women and the costs imposed on the firm as a consequence to avoid the possibility that women are discriminated against through mistaken stereotypes.[10]

A more direct reason for developing an equal-opportunities policy is the requirement for information if the employer is involved in proceedings before an industrial tribunal. Under Section 74 of the Sex Discrimination Act an aggrieved person can request an employer to set out, on a Section 74 form, relevant information and reasons for the treatment against which there is a complaint. Whilst there is no legal obligation on the employer to respond to such a request, failure to do so, or evasive responses, may be construed by tribunals as an indication of unlawful actions. Thus, in *Eaton v. Nuttall* the Employment Appeals Tribunal (E.A.T.) suggested that an employer was under an obligation to provide a tribunal with relevant and comprehensive information (including in this particular case adequate details of job evaluation and payment systems).

The House of Lords qualified this in *Nasse v. Science Research Council*, agreeing with the Court of Appeal that general disclosure orders regarding documents relating to job advertisements and interviews should ordinarily be avoided. Tribunals should only decide whether to allow complainants to see documents applied for after they have themselves examined them and irrelevant parts of such documents should be covered up. In a race case, though one of some relevance to sex discrimination, *Jalota v. Imperial Metal*

Industry (*Kynoch*) *Ltd*, E.A.T. refused on appeal a request by an employee for data on the ethnic composition of both staff and payroll employees on the grounds, amongst others, that this could in no way be relevant to the question whether the respondents were discriminating against the appellant.

It has also been suggested that a positive equal-opportunities programme may be an adequate defence for an employer in showing that he has taken reasonable steps to prevent individual employees from committing an unlawful act.[11] But in *Martin v. Tate and Lyle Food and Distribution Ltd*, where the union branch had maintained a policy of sex-based job demarcation, management had drawn up a document entitled 'Policy on sex discrimination' which was held by the tribunal to be 'an explicit and adequate statement of anti-discrimination policy within the framework of the Act'. Yet, the tribunal was not satisfied that 'positive and effective steps had been taken' fully to implement the policy among lower levels of management. A further consideration is that firms which do not take such initiatives may lay themselves open to the possibility of formal investigations by the E.O.C. and the issuing of non-discrimination notices as provided for in the S.D.A. In February 1977 the first such investigation was begun at the Luton site of Electrolux Ltd and by the Autumn of 1979 the E.O.C. had embarked on four further formal investigations relating to employment matters.[12]

Profit-maximising firms may well, however, be inclined to compare the costs of litigation and the probability of being caught with the costs of implementation of a positive equal-opportunities policy. Experience of the early years of equal-pay and sex-discrimination legislation suggests that the probability of being involved in a case (whether successfully pursued or otherwise) is relatively low and declining. Equal-pay claims fell from 1,742 in 1976 to 751 in 1977, 343 in 1978, 263 in 1979 and 91 in 1980, whilst the corresponding figures for sex discrimination cases were 243, 229, 171, 178 and 180 respectively.[13] In the first three years of the operation of the legislation, about 90 per cent of the equal-pay applications were made on the grounds of doing the same or broadly similar work as a person of the opposite sex and the remainder related to work rated as equivalent under a job-evaluation scheme. Of the 2,836 cases in this period, 161 were brought by men. Almost 60 per cent of the total applications were settled by conciliation or withdrawn prior to an industrial tribunal hearing: 11.6 per cent of complaints were upheld by an industrial tribunal and 29 per cent rejected (18.4 per cent on the grounds of not like or equivalent work, 6.7 per cent involving a material difference, 0.4 per cent not being the same employment and 3.5 per cent for other reasons). As far as the sex discrimination cases were concerned, a much higher proportion of cases were brought by men (almost 25 per cent). Of the total, 82.4 per cent of cases involved direct sex discrimination over the period, 10.7 per cent involved indirect sex discrimination, 4 per cent direct discrimination against married persons and 0.8 per cent indirect discrimination against married persons. The most common complaint was brought by employees regarding access to opportunities for promotion and other benefits, followed by employees in respect of dismissal and applicants for employment regarding refusal to engage or to offer employment. Of the cases, 59.1 per cent were cleared without a tribunal hearing (19.8 per cent by conciliated settlements); and 32.4 per cent of the 40.9 per cent of cases brought before a tribunal were dismissed. The explanations for the low incidence of cases compared to other forms of legislation such as unfair dismissal must at this stage remain a matter of conjecture. Does it imply that there is a lack of interest amongst the mass of individuals about discrimination, a lack of awareness of the terms of the legislation or that this legislation is narrowly drawn?

It would, however, be a mistake on the part of employers to assume that the legislative provisions may be ignored with impunity. If in the long run the male–female earnings differential fails to narrow appreciably there will undoubtedly be pressures for a widening of the scope of the legislation. In any event British law must conform to European legislation, as contained in Article 119 of the Treaty of Rome, which lays down equal pay for equal work. In February 1975 the Council of Ministers of the Community issued a directive which defined 'equal work' as meaning 'identical work or work of equal value', thus, potentially, widening considerably the effect of the Article, and a further directive was issued in February 1976 concerned with the equality of treatment for men and women with respect to access to employment, vocational training and promotion and working conditions. The European Commission took the view that the application of the principle of equal pay had still not been fully implemented in member states and in March 1978 announced its intention to initiate infringement procedures against seven member states (including the U.K.) on account of their failure to do so.

The first cases to be referred by British courts to the European Court of Justice illustrate how the effect of European law may be to widen considerably the scope of equality-of-opportunity legislation. In *Macarthys v. Smith* the Court of Appeal by a majority considered that the failure of the E.P.A. to allow comparisons with a predecessor in a job as opposed to an incumbent might be contrary to Article 119 and thus referred the matter to the European Court of Justice (E.C.J.). It was held by the E.C.J. that the principle in Article 119 of the Treaty of Rome was not confined to situations in which men and women were contemporaneously doing equal work for the same employer, and that the principle of equal pay applied also to a case where, having regard to the nature of the work undertaken, a woman had received less pay than a man who was employed prior to the woman and did equal work for the employer. In a second case to be referred, *Worringham and Humphries v. Lloyds Bank*, the Court of Appeal was of the view that the retirement exclusion of the E.P.A. might be in contravention of Article 119 since the latter contains no such exclusion clause. The problem was that the women's pension scheme was non-contributory until the age of 25, whilst men under 25 were obliged to contribute 5 per cent of their gross salary. To offset this the company added 5 per cent to the gross salary of the men. The E.C.J. held that this formed part of the employee's pay for the purposes of Article 119. Though there are relatively few schemes of this nature, the decision is likely to be expensive for the employer concerned.[14] In a third case where a woman received 10 per cent less pay per hour than male equivalents who worked a third longer (*Jenkins v. Kingsgate*) E.A.T. again referred the matter to the European Court.

Crucial questions here were whether part-time workers must be paid the same hourly rate as full-time workers irrespective of their value to the employer and whether the concept of indirect discrimination could be applied to the E.P.A. as well as the S.D.A. Here the E.C.J. found that it did not amount to unlawful discrimination to pay part-time women a lower hourly rate than their full-time male equivalents 'unless it is in reality merely an indirect way of reducing the pay of part-time workers on the grounds that that group of workers is composed exclusively or predominantly of women'.[15]

This decision does appear to extend the concept of indirect discrimination to the Equal Pay Act.

It seems highly likely that the scope of the legislation will be widened in the long run whether through the influence of European law or through changes to the British law.[16] This implies that managements may have to take more positive measures to tackle discrimination than in the past, at least as far as the majority of employers is concerned, and unions likewise will have to develop policies to keep up with the new developments.

2. Elements of an equal-opportunities policy

In its guidance on equal-opportunities policies and practices in employment, the E.O.C. suggested that the first step in implementing an equal-opportunities policy is its announcement at board level and incorporation into collective agreements and/or employee handbooks, but for success it is also necessary to ensure the commitment of senior staff and also any trade unions that may be involved. It is also important to ensure effective participation by employees perhaps through the institution of equal-opportunities committees in larger establishments. These points were amplified in the E.O.C.'s draft Code of Practice. For instance, the board of directors should issue a written statement setting out the organisation's commitment to equal opportunities and where there are recognised trade unions they should be consulted throughout the implementation stages of a policy so that they are fully committed to it. It should be noted that if the Code of Practice is implemented by Parliament the clauses contained in such a document will not be legally binding, but where relevant they may be taken into account in proceedings before an industrial tribunal.

A second step is to collect relevant statistics in relation to both the internal labour market of the firm and the external labour market. Broadly speaking the relevant statistics include distributions for grade, skill and pay differentiated by sex and marital status for each establishment or department.[17] It may also be necessary to collect separate data for manual and non-manual groups where these are clearly differentiated. If a company is to attempt to estimate earnings functions as discussed in Chapter 5 this will also require data for each individual employee (or a representative sample) relating to education, experience within the firm and elsewhere in the labour market, training undertaken and qualifications obtained. Where age-related pay scales apply, an age variable may be substituted for experience.[18] It is also necessary to maintain detailed absenteeism figures if it is to be argued that a failure to turn up for work, or lateness, makes a particular woman a less valuable employee. It can be seen therefore that an equal-opportunities policy requires a number of detailed statistics. We consider the issues of measurement in much greater detail in the following chapter.

The variables above are to be used to correct for differences in pay that are not a consequence of discrimination, but that is not to say that in all cases they will be relevant – they must be related to the requirements of the job. It will be recalled from section 3 of Chapter 2 that the Sex Discrimination Act defines indirect discrimination as a requirement or condition with which a considerably smaller proportion of one sex (or of married as opposed to unmarried persons) can comply, which is to the detriment of that group and which cannot be *justified* by the requirements of the job. Therefore, it is necessary to analyse jobs in order to ascertain what attributes they really do demand from workers rather than those which historically have been used to select workers for them. (The concept of indirect discrimination as well as direct discrimination already referred to in Chapter 1 and elsewhere is discussed further below.) It is also necessary to correct for motivational and related differences among workers and for productivity. First, certain groups of workers work different hours (in terms of both duration and times of work) and this is likely to influence earnings. In correcting for differences in hours, attention should be paid, however, to the possibility that certain groups are discriminated against, in terms of, for example, the opportunity to work overtime. Another area of significance could be non-pecuniary aspects of work. If, for instance, the unpleasantness of working conditions varies systematically among the various sex/marital status groups, allowance would have to be made for the possibility of compensating wage differentials, which may make discrimination hard to detect. If one estimates an earnings function in which occupational grade is added as an explanatory variable, one would then be comparing earnings in jobs for which variations in working conditions are limited, but this would have the effect of confining the study to an analysis of wage discrimination (differences in pay, given occupation). Consideration must also be given to variations in the input of effort. The presence of merit or payment-by-results systems does permit higher pay for better performance and hence will capture motivational differences amongst groups to the extent that sex biases in the reward system are absent. Where payment is made on a rigid time-rate basis, better performance may be rewarded through accelerated promotion as opposed to higher pay within occupational group.

Thus in comparing the various sex/marital status groups allowance must be made for systematic differences in performance among them. It is quite plausible to expect, at least given the traditional division of labour within the household (as already referred to in Chapter 3), that even in the absence of discrimination the experience or anticipation of having family responsibilities could influence orientation to work, albeit differently for men and women. Men, given their traditional role as primary family breadwinners, are likely to be more market-work oriented once married. Married women, on the other hand, will anticipate a shorter and more interrupted period in the labour force subsequent to marriage. As mentioned earlier, this will make it less worthwhile for them and their employers to invest in training. Single women, by contrast, are not likely to exhibit such a marked supply-side difference from single men as do married men from married women, though anticipation of marriage may influence many young women to acquire less on-the-job training than men with comparable education. Yet, we must bear in mind that some single women may have made a conscious decision to concentrate on a career and be more job-motivated than those single men who could be regarded as 'drifters'. Further, it is inadequate for employers to rest their case on such broad generalisations as those made above. In a case of alleged discrimination evidence on levels of productivity of particular individuals would be necessary to disprove the allegation that differences in pay and occupational level were based on sex. The same is true of other measures of motivation including absenteeism and turnover.

A third step, emphasised in the E.O.C.'s draft Code of Practice, in the development of such a policy is to carry out regular audits in order to monitor changes and analyse whether the objectives of the policy are being met. This would seem to require the updating of company statistics at least on an annual basis. One example is I.C.I.'s Code of Practice[19] which requires divisional managers to review annually patterns of male and female employment, including participation of each sex in training schemes, trends in promotion, applications and engagements for senior posts and applications for internally advertised jobs. Whilst there are no provisions for positive discrimination in favour of women in the British legislation, apart from the special training provisions of the Sex Discrimination Act, the logical development of equal-opportunities policies is seen most clearly in the u.s. affirmative action programme. This involves the setting up of goals and timetables for employment in job categories where women have been 'under-utilised'. Here goals are distinguished from quotas (which are unlawful). What is implied is an attempt to estimate what an employer's workforce would look like had there been no unlawful discrimination in the past.[20] The crucial question is, however, what is the expected proportion of women in each occupational group and at each level of pay in the absence of discrimination? The e.o.c. seems to imply in its Guidance that it is simply a question of examining the means of the distributions and attempting to correct for any major disparities thus revealed. As we show in Chapter 5, however, it can be highly misleading to make judgements on the basis of means, when male and female groups diverge considerably in terms of their personal characteristics. The earnings function approach adopted in this book, despite the problems discussed earlier, can take us much further in attempting to judge how far firms have failed to attain reasonable targets for equality of opportunity.

A further problem is to establish what is the relevant population of women with respect to recruitment to a particular plant or occupation within it. We may define the local labour market of a firm as that geographical area containing those members of the labour force (or potential members of the labour force) whom a firm believes it can induce to enter its employment under certain conditions. However, there is reason to believe that this labour market will be different for men and women and this will be particularly true in the case of married women. Because of child-care commitments, wives tend to search for jobs closer to home than do husbands. Further, if the husband's potential earnings are higher than those of the wife and the family possesses one car, a possible outcome is that the husband will travel to work by car and the wife by public transport or other means, thereby confirming the higher potential earnings for the husband. Given this fact, it is an over-simplification to assume that a firm's female–male employment ratio will be in line with the female labour-force participation rate in a given labour-market area. Particularly, if a firm is located in a relatively inaccessible area, it is likely to have a preponderance of male applicants for jobs.

Further, where jobs require specific skills we need to know the number of women with relevant skills in the labour-market area. In *Price v. Civil Service Commission* E.A.T. considered that the appropriate pool was all qualified men and women rather than the entire population. As far as certain professional groups, such as graduates, are concerned, we might regard the relevant labour market as the whole economy, or even the E.E.C., and it is relatively straightforward to estimate the expected percentage of females on the basis of the percentage of graduates who are female. Even here, there could be complications however. Suppose, for instance, graduate men tend to marry graduate women. Once the husband gains a potential advantage in labour-market earnings, as may happen if the wife temporarily leaves the labour market to raise children, job changes will be dictated by the husband, thereby reducing the potential job-search area of the wife. These complications can explain why the United States courts, for instance, have fallen back on rules of thumb such as the percentage of a minority group in the total population of a city, Standard Metropolitan Statistical Area, state or region.

As far as the individual firm is concerned it would seem appropriate, in view of the above problems, to confine its attention to the ratio of job-applicants of each sex to appointees (bearing in mind potential biases caused by particular methods of recruitment, as outlined below) and the relative rates of advancement of each sex within the department, establishment or enterprise.

Yet another problem arises from the hidden assumption of equal-opportunities legislation that there already exists equal pay among men for clearly defined occupational groups. Numerous labour-market studies have in fact demonstrated that there is a very wide spread of earnings for homogeneous groups within local labour markets, making it uncertain which comparison is appropriate between women and men. In part, differences arise from the substantial differences in earnings among firms and plants for particular occupations. This cannot be remedied by existing legislation, which is concerned only with comparisons made within parts of the same or associated employer where common terms and conditions of employment apply. However, a recent study has shown that intra-plant earnings dispersion is just as significant as inter-plant dispersion. The study compared separately standard weekly earnings for unskilled and semi-skilled male manual production workers in the engineering industry and used relatively well defined local labour-market areas.[21] This raises questions as to how far market forces are to be constrained by the requirements for equality of opportunity. In the case of *Fletcher v. Clay Cross (Quarry Services) Ltd* it had been decided by E.A.T. that where an employer pays a worker more for doing the same work because the person concerned had been earning more in his previous employment and would not come for less, that this was a material difference, genuinely due to some factor other than sex. However, in the Court of Appeal, Lord Denning stated that acceptance of the above argument would make the E.P.A. a 'dead letter'. Intention of the employer was irrelevant, and consequently market forces do not constitute a material difference within the Act.[22] This would seem to have significant implications for any attempts to make deviations from established wage structures on an individual basis in order to make firms more competitive in the labour market.

3. Some practical aspects of equal-opportunities legislation

British equal-opportunities legislation has been in operation since the end of 1975 and a substantial body of case law has now been built up which provides guidelines for dealing with areas of difficulty. Equal opportunity covers (a) entry into the firm or organisation, (b) promotion within it, (c) the level of pay, holding occupation constant, and (d) dismissal or acts to the detriment of workers. It is necessary to examine each of these aspects in turn.

(a) Entry into the firm

The legislation requires that job advertisements should neither state nor imply that jobs are open to members of one sex only (except in the case of genuine occupational qualifications). But there is also evidence that the method of filling vacancies will itself help to determine whether applicants from one sex or the other predominate. Thus the 1977 General Household Survey shows that of males aged 16 and over in their present job for less than twelve months 16 per cent first heard about their present job from an employment office, as opposed to 10 per cent of females; 12 per cent as opposed to 4 per cent heard from a private employment agency; 23 per cent as opposed to 26 per cent heard from an advertisement; 33 per cent as opposed to 38 per cent heard from friends and relatives; and 22 per cent as opposed to 19 per cent heard by direct approach to the employer. Whilst the above may not be wholly reflected in actual recruitment methods, the importance of form of recruitment has been borne out in a formal investigation, carried out by the Commission for Racial Equality, of F. Broomfield Ltd, a London firm of bakers and confectioners, where it was suggested that word-of-mouth recruitment of drivers was a form of indirect discrimination. The E.O.C.'s draft code of practice also suggests that recruitment solely or primarily by word of mouth in a workforce which is predominantly of one sex should be avoided.

As the I.P.M. report[23] points out, firms must ensure that individuals in key posts do not operate their own unofficial recruitment policies to screen out candidates they regard as undesirable, even though an official equal-opportunities policy is applied by their own organisation in general. Under section 41(1) of the Sex Discrimination Act employers are responsible for such discrimination. Key occupations in this respect are gatekeepers, receptionists, telephonists, personnel department secretaries, supervisors and line managers and the E.O.C.'s draft Code suggests that training and guidance should be provided for such personnel to ensure that they understand their responsibilities in relation to the organisation's own policy and the law. It should be emphasised again that, according to the General Household Survey, over 20 per cent of employees first sought their present job by a direct approach to the employer. Therefore, it is important that this section of the workforce in particular is given clear instructions on equality of opportunity policies within the organisation.

Care needs to be taken to ensure that interviews are seen to be fair by those invited to attend. Given the possibility of a claim of discriminatory treatment, however remote, it seems prudent to retain the application forms of unsuccessful candidates for a reasonable length of time. These may also be useful for monitoring recruitment policies. As our study of clerical vacancies (to which further reference will be made in Chapter 6) reveals, the sex of the previous job incumbent seems strongly to influence the sex of the new appointee. In other words, there may be a tendency among interviewers to look for replacements with the same characteristics as the previous job-holder, with the chances of perpetuating job stereotypes and discrimination. The E.O.C.'s draft Code of Practice suggests that all applications should be processed in the same manner and separate lists of male, female, married and single applicants should be avoided; that records of interviews should be kept, wherever practicable, showing why applicants were or were not selected; that where tests are used care should be taken to avoid irrelevant bias towards either sex; and finally that questions relating to marriage or family intentions should not be asked. Questions at the interview concerning sex, marital status or family circumstances could well be held to imply discriminatory behaviour. However, in *Saunders v. Richmond-upon-Thames Borough Council* E.A.T. did not consider that it was unlawful to ask a female applicant for a golf-professional vacancy such questions as whether men would respond as well to a female as to a male golf professional or whether she would be able to control disputes over starting times. Questions also arise as to how much seniority should be given to married women who return to work after an absence. The E.O.C. has acknowledged that it would 'not be fair or practicable for her to be placed immediately at the level she would have attained if she had been at work continuously'[24] and this accords with human capital theory.

As far as indirect discrimination is concerned, one of the most important cases so far, *Price v. Civil Service Commission*, involved the question of age limits. It appears that age limits should not be unduly restrictive. The case itself related to the age barrier of 28 for direct entry into the Executive Officer grade which made it harder in practice for women to comply than men. Whilst it was accepted that it was desirable to ensure that a proportion of direct-entry entrants to the grade in question was drawn from the lower age groups in order to maintain a balanced career structure, it was held that there were alternative ways of achieving this that the defendants had not considered and which were non-discriminatory.[25] The I.P.M. Joint Standing Committee[26] has also suggested that setting criteria substantially in excess of the real requirements of the job may also infringe the indirect discrimination clauses of the legislation, as in the case in the United States following the Griggs judgement where it was found that apparently neutral practices which tended to perpetuate the effects of past discrimination were unlawful. However, such behaviour may simply represent an attempt by employers to cream the market, paying higher wages to obtain higher quality

46

labour. This may be particularly appropriate in well-developed internal labour markets where recruitment is essentially being made for a sequence of jobs with promotion possibilities rather than merely for the entry grade. Whether this approach to selection would be held to be unlawful under these circumstances remains to be determined.

As noted earlier, where during the previous 12 months there have been no (or comparatively few) persons of one sex doing a particular type of work, it is permissible to give special encouragement to members of that group to enter training. One example of this is the scholarship offered since 1976 by the Engineering Industry Training Board, designed exclusively to introduce girls into industry as engineering technicians.[27] That this is an exception to the general rule is indicated by the fact that, in the survey of 500 companies, the E.O.C. found only seven employees who had made use of positive discrimination (mainly in the management area) as allowed under section 48 of the S.D.A. How far this represents self-selection by women themselves is uncertain.

(b) Promotion

It is invariably found to be the case that few women reach the most senior posts in any establishment or enterprise. For example the Equal Pay and Opportunity Project at the London School of Economics[28] found that, in nine of the twenty-six companies investigated, women were blocked from better-paid or higher-grade jobs because of lifting requirements; in seven women were excluded from better-paid or career jobs because of their alleged inability to do shift-work or overtime; and in many cases the use of traditional promotion paths (e.g. promotion to supervision and management from the technical or shop floor rather than clerical or administrative area) all but eliminated women.[29] Such an issue arose in *Bath v. British Airways Overhaul Ltd.* A female aircraft component worker was rejected for promotion to production assistant on the grounds that she did not possess acceptable trade or storekeeping experience. In fact, out of 793 storemen employed, only one was a woman. The tribunal rejected the employer's argument that it would take 30 months to train an experienced aircraft component worker to become a production assistant, as opposed to only 12 for a senior storekeeper, on the grounds that the former would be capable of doing useful and productive work during the training period. It is also important to ensure in such cases that women are not barred on the basis of mistaken stereotypes. For instance, have technological changes reduced the burden of lifting? And, are women (or a substantial number of them) prepared to work overtime? If so, companies may well be in breach of the legislation.

It is also necessary to guard against the possibility that the effects of earlier discriminatory practices continue to operate to the detriment of women. In *Steel v. Post Office* a policy of promotion by seniority was found to have adversely affected certain women who until 1975 had been barred from acquiring 'permanent' status with consequent seniority rights. E.A.T. found that this requirement could not be justified and constituted a *prima facie* case of indirect discrimination. As Glucklich and Povall[30] point out, it may not be sufficient, therefore, for an employer to abolish a previously discriminatory policy, if the effects of that policy continue to be felt by members of the workforce.[31]

The study of clerical vacancies referred to above (see also Chapter 6) points to one reason why women might find promotion difficult. Several respondents stated that supervision of males by females would be a problem because, where there was a mixed workforce, males disliked being supervised by a woman and even women themselves did not seem to like supervising men. It would appear therefore, to the extent that such attitudes are prevalent, that women's chances of promotion are greatest where the entire workforce or work-group is female.

(c) *The level of pay given occupation*

The E.P.A. requires equality for the same or broadly similar ('like') work or for work rated as equivalent under a job-evaluation scheme with regard to persons engaged by a particular or associated employer where common terms and conditions of employment apply. Where no such clause exists an equality clause is implied as existing in the contract of each worker, save where there is a material difference in the work being undertaken. There are also exclusion clauses relating to laws regulating the employment of women, terms providing special treatment for women by reason of pregnancy or childbirth and terms related to death or retirement.

Whether work can legally be described as 'like' depends upon a detailed knowledge of the work being undertaken. Initially the burden of proof is on the applicant to show that she (he) is engaged on like work with a particular man (woman) or group of men (women). What the men and women actually do, and how often, appears to be important, rather than what might be stated in the contract of employment. But, if a tribunal decides that work is the same or broadly similar, the next stage is to ask whether there are any differences of a practical importance – the sort of thing one might expect to be reflected in a contract of employment. Finally, it is necessary to determine whether or not any differences in remuneration are genuinely due to a material difference (other than that of sex) and here the burden of proof rests upon the employer. Initially, it was suggested that this was a 'very heavy burden' but more recently in *Vulcan v. Wade* it has been suggested that it is the ordinary burden of proof in civil cases (i.e. on the balance of probabilities).

It is important to emphasise that a case will fail if there are no men doing 'like' work. Thus, in *Waddington v. Leicester Council for Voluntary Service* the complainant, who was paid less than someone she had helped to select and for whom she was responsible, failed because her work, being wider and carrying greater responsibility, was not the same or broadly similar. In this respect the *Macarthys v. Smith* case, to which reference has been made earlier, is important as it has set a precedent for comparisons to be made with male (or female) workers who have been previously employed on the same job. E.A.T. has suggested that where, after a detailed examination of the duties of the parties and contracts of employment, it remains uncertain whether the work done is 'like' work, factory or site visits should be organised.

Given that it is shown by the complainant that work is 'like' or 'equivalent', what might constitute a material difference? It appears from cases so far that, provided criteria are objectively chosen, the pay gap is wholly due to material difference and that if the difference is not sex-based, factors such as merit, general maturity, potential contribution to the job, qualifications and seniority might constitute a material difference. But much depends on the circumstances. For instance, in *Handley v. Mono*, E.A.T. decided that part-time work could constitute a material difference. But there were very special circumstances here, such as the fact that the difference in hours was substantial, all full-time workers (who included women) were treated alike regardless of sex, the complainant was entitled to enhanced overtime rates after working fewer hours than full-timers and her machine was idle whilst she was not at work, thereby reducing her overall value. Again, in *National Coal Board v. Sherwin and Spruce* E.A.T. considered that the time at which work was done was immaterial if it was 'like' work. Thus, the disadvantage of night-work could be compensated by the payment of a night-shift premium rather than a higher basic rate. However, it was suggested that if the same work done at night involved genuine differences such as additional duties or responsibilities this may amount to a material difference. Age may justify higher pay if it affects ability to work. Thus in *White v. Scot Bowyers Ltd* the tribunal held that the age difference of three years between a man and a woman justified a 6 per cent difference in salaries. Yet in *West v. Burroughs Machines Ltd* an age gap of 33 years was held not to justify a 20 per cent pay differential because the man concerned was no more experienced at the work he was then doing than the complainant. Similarly, length of service will justify differences in pay provided it can be shown that it influences performance.

The extent to which women may claim comparison with men may be considerably widened where a system of job evaluation has been implemented. In the E.O.C.'s survey of 500 firms it was found that 15 per cent of respondents had a full job-evaluation scheme, 44 per cent had partial job evaluation, 2 per cent were about to introduce such a scheme and only 10 per cent had no scheme at all.[32]

Job evaluation has been defined as 'the comparison of jobs by formal and systematic procedures, set down on paper and adhered to as distinct from rule of thumb methods in order, after analysis, to determine the relative position of one job to another in the wage or salary hierarchy'.[33] One is essentially rating the job rather than the worker, but it has been suggested that in some cases the content of a job may depend on an individual employee and what he or she makes of it.[34] Then it is particularly important to ensure that job descriptions are accurate. Information about jobs can be collected via observations, interviews, questionnaires, checklists and supervisory conferences. Excessive reliance on supervisory interview could result in biased job descriptions if they are partly influenced by perceptions about the persons who currently hold the job (e.g. male or female) rather than the job content.

Though job evaluation is supposed to be objective it is perhaps more accurately defined as an objective procedure that deals partly with subjective values. There are a large number of types of job-evaluation scheme in operation, including points rating, factor comparison, grading and ranking. Commonly, in the more analytical of these schemes, factors such as skill, responsibility, mental effort, physical effort and working conditions are taken into consideration, and the relative position given to a particular job within the hierarchy of jobs very much depends on the weighting given to each of these factors. In order to be taken into account by an industrial tribunal a job-evaluation study must be valid, which was defined by E.A.T. in *Paton Ltd v. Nuttall* as meaning 'a study satisfying the test of being thorough in analysis and capable of impartial application'. It should, it appears from *England v. Borough of Bromley*, also be complete and objective and, by its application, enable all factors of importance in relation to work to be taken into account, making it unnecessary for employers or their representatives to make subjective judgements upon the work content (rather a tall order in view of the above discussion).

A job-evaluation scheme does not, however, have to be implemented, before it is valid. In *O'Brien v. Sim-Chem Ltd* the House of Lords held that a job-evaluation study has been completed when the stage has been reached at which an employee can show his or her job has been evaluated, even if the terms of employment have not yet been revised to incorporate the findings. If job evaluation is undertaken it must not be weighted unfairly in favour of one sex or the other, nor may one group be paid more than another where they are rated as equal under such a scheme. However, tribunals are not entitled to consider whether in their view job evaluation should have been conducted differently (e.g. based on different factors). Thus, in *Brown and Mitchell v. John Maddock Ltd* an independent consultant gave evidence for the applicants regarding a job-evaluation scheme based on the paired comparisons method, which had been jointly agreed by management and union. He alleged that the paired comparisons method was crude and lacking in finesse, that the scheme had an anti-feminist bias and that there were fundamental errors in the job descriptions. None the less the tribunal was satisfied that the job evaluation was valid. The legislation is concerned with equality of treatment and not about the quality of management. Nor may women argue that female attributes such as dexterity should have been awarded higher points than male attributes such as strength. In *Johnson v. Bridon Fibres and Plastics* points allocation was held to be a matter for negotiation between the employer and trade unions. However, a failure to include trade unions or women in the development of a job-evaluation scheme might be held to imply a lack of impartiality.

A.C.A.S. has suggested that job-evaluation committees should include members of both sexes where appropriate.[35] Yet one investigation of 94 organisations which had implemented job evaluation for manual employees found that, in 43 of them employing female manual workers, no women sat either on the steering committees or on the evaluation panels. Of the remaining 37 companies employing women, most had selected one woman to sit on the evaluation panel.

The E.O.C. in its first annual report expressed concern that tribunals had been inconsistent in examining the various schemes in operation and considered that the results of such schemes had been accepted or rejected without clear reasons. In its second report it drew attention to the fact that it was unable to provide assistance to women affected by schemes which gave greater emphasis to predominantly male attributes to the detriment of female attributes, and suggested that it would be helpful if suspect schemes could be referred to the Central Arbitration Committee for examination. Further, it announced its intention to issue guidance and ultimately recommend a Code of Practice on job evaluation and with this in mind a Working Party was set up in July 1978. Presumably the first task for such a body would be to examine the reasons why, in the majority of cases, a far greater proportion of jobs undertaken mainly or wholly by women are placed, by most job-evaluation schemes, at or near the bottom of the job hierarchy. One study[36] has suggested that the answer lies in the fact that job evaluation is based upon subjective procedures, which in turn are influenced by political considerations and personal values as much as by economic and technological factors. Thus neither management nor male workers would see it as being in their interests to make radical alterations to the existing hierarchy of jobs. Also, the low status of 'women's work' may be reflected in the relative value of jobs, as determined under the job-evaluation scheme. The E.O.C. concluded that, amongst other things, it was necessary to give manual dexterity, accuracy and concentration (all attributes of 'women's work') a comparable weighting to physical effort and strength (attributes of 'men's work').

This neglects the fact, however, that weighting will tend to reflect the value placed on any attribute by the market and if male characteristics are in short supply relative to demand, when compared with female attributes, then a higher price will be placed upon them. This is one reason why job-evaluation schemes are unlikely to depart markedly from the *status quo* in the determination of the relative worth of jobs.

(d) Detrimental acts and dismissal

The S.D.A. also lays down that there must be equality of treatment with respect to acts which are to the detriment of workers, such as redundancy or dismissal. Thus in *McKenna v. U.D.S. Tailoring Ltd* a tribunal confirmed that it was unfair to make a woman redundant before a man with three years' less service and in spite of a nationally agreed procedure. Women may be placed under a particular disadvantage through the operation of 'last-in, first-out' procedures for determining which workers will be laid off first when there is a temporary or permanent decline in demand. Since women tend on average to have less seniority than men, they will tend to be disproportionately affected by such procedures. It remains to be determined whether this would be regarded by the courts as indirect discrimination. In its draft Code of Practice the E.O.C. recommended that alternatives should at least be considered where a redundancy arrangement was likely to have a disproportionate effect on one sex, and went on to state that 'arrangements which laid off all part-time workers first should be avoided. It could constitute unlawful discrimination since it would mean that most of those made redundant are women. A voluntary redundancy arrangement might be considered as an alternative.'

The questions of a failure to provide the same benefits to one sex as to the other arose in *Automotive Products Ltd v. Peake*. E.A.T. considered that women being allowed to leave work five minutes before the men for reasons of good administration and safety amounted to discrimination against men. The Court of Appeal, however, refused to accept that the five-minute rule was either less or more favourable treatment (referring in passing to questions of chivalry) because the matter was not sufficiently substantial. The E.O.C. expressed concern at this ruling as it had previously been understood that intention and motive were irrelevant in determining whether or not there had been discrimination. In another Court of Appeal case, *Jeremiah v. Ministry of Defence*, Lord Denning referred to the above case and stated that he now felt that the earlier decision was correct only on the *de minimis* principle (trifles) and not on the question of chivalry and administrative practice. The decision here seems to confirm that motive is irrelevant in a sex discrimination case. In the Jeremiah case the Court of Appeal upheld the decision of E.A.T. that payment for obnoxious work did not prevent the discrimination from being a detriment. It would appear therefore that it is a dangerous procedure to withhold unpleasant jobs from women, even if extra recompense is given to men who perform them.[37] E.A.T. has recently decided that it is not direct sex discrimination to dismiss a woman because she is pregnant (*Turley v. Allders Dept. Stores Ltd*).[38] The majority ruled that there is no male equivalent to a pregnant woman, a like-for-like comparison being a requirement for both direct and indirect discrimination, whilst the dissenting view was that pregnancy was a medical condition and a male might require time off during the course of the year for such a reason. In turn this raises the question whether it might be lawful to reject an applicant for a job on the basis that she may in due course have a child. However, in overturning a tribunal decision, E.A.T. in *Hurley v. Mustoe* found that a policy not to employ women with young children cannot be justified on the grounds that some women with young children are unreliable.[39] A blanket condition, as in this case, was not *necessary* to achieve reliability, as it was possible to assess each individual applicant separately. Over a quarter of cases so far brought under the Sex Discrimination Act have concerned the question of dismissal and this is clearly an important area of the legislation.

4. Conclusion

It appears that legislation has a limited effect in altering the position of women relative to men in the labour market. This is particularly so because the area of comparison is restricted. For this reason, and because the number of cases brought under the Equal Pay Act is declining, and under the Sex Discrimination Act is static, an intensification of activity by the E.O.C. is likely to result. Recognising the importance of job segregation, the E.O.C. revealed in its third annual report that it was concentrating its attention on ways in which this might be remedied through actions by managements and unions together, backed up by formal investigations and research enquiries. The Commission's early priorities had been to scrutinise pay structures and job-evaluation schemes, equality of opportunity in promotion, training and recruitment, and the provision of re-entry training for women returning to work and to review the protective legislation in so far as it related to women. By its second report, a more interventionist role had been initiated as far as research was concerned. This involved following up cases, such as successful claims of unequal treatment, in order to trace cases of persistent discrimination, where tribunals had made specific recommendations, and where it appeared from the tribunal's decision that job segregation had been practised. It also involved contacting complainants who had at some stage withdrawn their application to have their case heard by a tribunal. It is to be expected that this more positive approach will be intensified as exemplified by the development of the draft Code of Practice. Further, the Commission has already announced its intention to enquire more deeply into the attitudes and practices of trade unions.[40] To this end the E.O.C. is currently conducting a survey of equality of opportunities between the sexes within unions. A questionnaire sent to the unions requests information on membership numbers, qualifications for membership, whether the union has an equality-of-opportunities policy and the degree of female participation in union activities. In parallel with this it is conducting a number of joint exercises with employers in both the private and public sectors.

In reviewing the scope of the legislation the E.O.C. has drawn attention to the rigidity of the Equal Pay Act, which does not, for instance, allow comparisons of equal value in the absence of job evaluation. Further, it notes that the Department of Employment has taken the view that collective agreements must contain a specific reference to 'male' and/or 'female' terms and conditions before they can be referred to the Central Arbitration Committee. The Commission endorses the less restricted view of the latter body and is considering proposals for the reform of the law in this direction. Other proposals the E.O.C. has made to the Home Secretary are equal treatment for men and women in all occupational and state pension schemes; common retirement ages for men and women; the addition of family status into the Sex Discrimination Act; the shifting of the burden of evidence under that Act to the alleged discriminator once

55

less favourable treatment is shown; the recruitment of women only (or men only) as well as use of existing employees for training for jobs in which there are comparatively few women (or men); and the granting to tribunals of the power to order re-employment as well as compensation.

The implications of these developments for managements and trade unions would appear to be threefold. First, the parties need to ensure that they are as familiar as possible with the precise terms of the legislation so that they do not practise discrimination through ignorance. Second, detailed information is required on the distribution of men and women in each enterprise and this requires the compilation of detailed statistics on a regular basis. Third, it would be advantageous to develop an equal-opportunities policy, which explicitly incorporates the methodology explained in detail in the next chapter, and monitors on a regular basis the extent to which objectives are being met.

5

Measuring discrimination at the place of work

Chapter 3 examined the sex differential in the economy as a whole and Chapter 4 considered the legal implications of discrimination. The present chapter discusses the analysis of discrimination at the place of work. There are a number of reasons for arguing that such an approach is just as or even more important than a more global approach. First, managers, workers and trade unionists are likely to be most concerned with any differential treatment which takes place within the individual firm or establishment. As discussed in the previous chapter, both the Equal Pay Act and Sex Discrimination Act are mainly directed towards the establishment. For instance, group differences in wage rates for similar occupations or in occupational distributions within an industry, or over the economy as a whole, do not constitute an infringement of the legislation. Further, although the law, at least as regards sex discrimination, is primarily concerned with individual grievances, the tests we suggest are widely applicable using information readily available to management. They may therefore serve as an important screen in assessing whether there appears to be a difference in treatment between the sexes, and hence whether they can direct attention to the point at which the employer needs to take action. A second related point is that much more relevant data will be available at the firm or establishment level, to control for differences in productivity-enhancing attributes of individuals. Third, on a more general note, as Higgs has emphasised,[1] economists who analyse discrimination have mainly been concerned with the behaviour of firms in the labour market. The analysis has largely concentrated on different treatment within the individual firm and, although this may be criticised as narrow, it is an important first step in assessing the extent of the problem and providing means for its solution. For these reasons it is important that evidence obtained is firm-specific. We are therefore going to make some suggestions about the nature, form and use which might be made of data collected by an individual enterprise or organisation.

1. Reasons for differences in average earnings between males and females within the organisation

To analyse differences in earnings within an organisation it is necessary to identify a decision-making unit which has the discretion to determine the operation and implementation of a wages and employment policy. Whether this is at firm or plant level depends on the organisational structure of the firm. Having established such a unit, observations on earnings in any given time period are likely to reveal differences between males and females on average. In section 2 of Chapter 4 we discussed such differences in some detail, and these may be summarised as follows: (i) hours of work, (ii) patterns of work – e.g. shift-work, payment-by-results, (iii) job assignments, (iv) skills and other wage-enhancing characteristics such as seniority in an incremental system, (v) pay for the same job for workers of equal productivity. Discrimination by the employer or fellow employees can affect any of these factors. As noted earlier, they are also affected by discriminatory influences in society at large such as access to education and role characterisation as well as decisions taken in the light of the division of labour in the household, whether dictatorially imposed by one party or mutually determined.[2]

Many researchers avoid the problem of differences in hours of work by concentrating on the wage rate of full-time workers rather than hourly or weekly earnings. Given that actual hours worked are the result of the interaction of supply and demand this is probably a reasonable simplification. If hours of work do differ systematically between males and females it is not necessarily evidence of discrimination. But the possibility of using hours of work and overtime earnings as a discriminatory device should not be overlooked in any individual study.

Items (iii), (iv) and (v) on the list are very closely interconnected; any allocation of earnings differences between them is relatively arbitrary. Much hinges on the definition of the job assignment and to a large extent this may be determined by the skill content of the job. Taken to its extreme all wage discrimination is simply job discrimination, since tasks with different wages can be defined as different jobs. Nevertheless most practical payments systems will have some clear discontinuities with different levels of job and different, possibly overlapping, pay scales. For instance, in the university sector, which has been the subject of much study, particularly in the United States,[3] the structure of teaching consists of assistant, associate and full professor or, in the U.K., lecturer, senior lecturer/reader and professor. The issue is closely related to the distinction between vertical and horizontal occupational segregation referred to in Chapter 2.[4]

Where there are different level jobs within an enterprise there are two key issues: (i) the level to which the individual is assigned on being hired; and (ii) promotion or re-assignment from one level to another. The institutional framework should be taken as given and access to job levels within this may be the principal way through which discrimination is exercised and perpetuated. Such issues will be discussed more fully in the following chapter.

Abstracting from the problems involved with different job levels, it is necessary to consider how one would seek to establish how important discrimination is within a particular job in a specific organisation. There are a number of different questions concerned here: (i) Is there any evidence that the organisation discriminates in general against (or in favour of) women? (ii) What is the significance and magnitude of such discrimination if it exists? (iii) Is there any evidence of discrimination against any one particular individual?

It is necessary to distinguish carefully between the approach that might be adopted by an economist or other social scientist and that likely to be followed by a lawyer as noted in Chapter 2. The law, and therefore the lawyer, is often primarily concerned with the position of a particular individual. Thus, as discussed in Chapter 4, one of the major remedies under the Sex Discrimination Act in Britain is the right of an individual to take his or her specific complaint to an industrial tribunal. The tribunal will only be concerned with the rights or wrongs in that particular case. The tools of the economist, on the other hand, are more appropriate for dealing with the general issue. As regards legislation, the approach we adopt is perhaps more appropriate for seeking an anti-discrimination notice by the Equal Opportunities Commission. Nevertheless the framework offered can also be used as supporting evidence in any individual case.

Further, as regards the law, all that may be required is a negative or affirmative answer to the question of the existence of discrimination. The precise magnitude may be irrelevant but would form the basis for any assessment of the possible effects of anti-discrimination legislation[5] and would give the firm some idea of the size of any likely costs imposed by the removal of discrimination.

2. The basic approach

There is no effective procedure for directly assessing the existence and extent of discrimination. However, the procedure adopted in legal cases in relation to individuals can be applied to the general sphere. If two people, identical apart from sex, are treated differently either in terms of the job assignment or in wages, given the job assignment, the existence of sex discrimination may be inferred. But what is meant by 'identical'? At the extreme is the case implied by the taste-based theories of discrimination discussed in Chapter 2. In this model individuals are assumed identical, i.e. they are perfect substitutes, but they receive different wages. Identical in this sense means equally productive. But how can this be made operational in the real world? It is necessary to find some index of productivity and then compare the treatment of individuals with the same value for the index. Productivity is, however, rather difficult to observe, particularly for an outside researcher, as noted in the work of Battalio *et al.*, referred to earlier. There have been very few attempts to obtain any direct estimate of productivity, and this is a possible avenue for further research. It would be possible to conduct further laboratory experiments but these may not always be a reliable guide to actual work performance. In addition the problem is complex because specific attention has to be paid to the time dimension – it is not just present but also future performance that is relevant. The rational employer would have to take appropriate account of the likely future contribution of an individual, which must include an assessment of the probability that he or she will leave the firm. The problems of information are substantial and it is not surprising that employers are likely to resort to group norms and rules of thumb in their employment decisions.[6]

Given the absence of any direct information on productivity, can anything be done to offset this disadvantage? Economists now turn to their theories of the operation of the labour market amongst which the marginal-productivity approach has been dominant.

Under competitive conditions workers will be paid the value of their marginal product, i.e. the value of their additional contribution to output. If, on the other hand, the final product is produced under non-competitive conditions, workers will be paid the value of their addition to the total revenue of the enterprise. In each case, observation of the wage will give a suitable indicator of net productivity where due allowance is made for training and other costs of employment.[7] It is not necessary to insist on a strict link between the wage and net marginal product as long as there is a strictly increasing monotonic relationship between wages and productivity such that the more productive individuals are paid more. Hence the wage can be taken as an index of performance as evaluated by the employer. Given access to suitable information this is readily observable by the researcher or the firm itself. Productivity is presumed to be a function of a number of characteristics of the worker. Thus, for example, it might be taken that more highly educated or more highly trained workers are more productive. In the former case we can abstract from any causal link between education and productivity, as it does not matter for the present purposes whether education directly improves performance or merely identifies individuals who are inherently more productive.[8] It is the presumed link between productivity and earnings which has led economists to concentrate on the estimation of wage or earnings functions where the wage rate is postulated as having some relationship to the characteristics of the worker.

Broadly, there are two ways of measuring an earnings function: one is first to obtain data on any characteristics which might be thought to be relevant and then experiment with various combinations of the variables and alternative functional forms and finally choose the model which best fits the data. This method is called data-mining and is essentially *ad hoc*. The alternative is to develop some model of the behaviour of the economic agents which may be able to reveal the appropriate variables and the form of the equation.

3. Investment in human capital and earnings

One popular analysis of the earnings function is that of the human-capital school. This views the productivity, and hence wage, of the individual as being largely under his or her own control. Improvements can be made through specific decisions such as staying in education beyond the compulsory minimum school-leaving age or by acquiring training whilst at work (on-the-job training). The acquisition of skills through such processes is not costless and in particular involves some sacrifice of current income in order to reap benefits in the future. This proposition perhaps needs further explanation since in Britain tuition fees are paid by the state for full-time domestic students, who also receive maintenance grants which are subject to a parental contribution. For most British students, further education involves no direct cash outlay and no necessity to take out long-term loans. In what sense, therefore, are there any costs to the individual? The costs involved are an opportunity cost primarily reflecting the potential earnings forgone during the voluntary years at school, college or university. For typical university graduates, who take two years to study 'A' levels and a further three years on a first degree, such costs may be sizeable. Just as undertaking current costs for an expected future return is an act of investment so, too, is a firm using some of its current income to build a new factory. As far as education or training is concerned the investment creates capital in the form of human capital.

Human capital investment by the individual does not necessarily cease on completion of schooling. The individual may wish to continue to forgo some part of his earnings capacity, taking lower current earnings in order to benefit from higher earnings later in life. Here we are concerned with the behaviour of the individual over the life-cycle.[9] As the worker ages he gets nearer to retirement, and the number of years over which he can obtain a return on his investment shortens. We would, therefore, expect the individual to devote less and less time to investment – a smaller fraction of his earnings capacity – as he gets older. A common assumption is that the fraction of earnings capacity devoted to investment declines linearly with age. Such an assumption yields the standard human capital earnings function[10] where the log of earnings is a function of years of schooling, experience, experience squared and a number of other variables, i.e.

$$\ln Y_i = f(s_i, t_i, t_i^2, Z_i)$$

where Y_i is the observed earnings of the ith individual;

s_i is the years of schooling;

t_i is years of work experience;

Z_i is a vector of other variables.

One important point to notice is that the relevant variable is a measure of work experience. In many data sets this is not available. It is frequently approximated by subtracting years of schooling and pre-school years from age, as a measure of potential work experience. Where labour-market experience is discontinuous such a measure is inadequate and this applies with particular force to women who may frequently experience a spell out of employment whilst they look after young children.[11] Further, the other variables included in any particular empirical study tend to differ according to the data set being used. A major problem concerns the inclusion, or exclusion, of a variable measuring the ability of an individual and the effect this has on the estimation of the equation.[12] Also, years of schooling is an extremely crude proxy for education since quality varies substantially between schools, and some studies include an additional variable purporting to measure quality differences.[13]

Not all training is paid for by the worker himself. The literature distinguishes between general and specific training.[14] Completely general training raises the productivity of the worker equally in all firms. It would be irrational for a profit-maximising firm to invest in the creation of completely general skills, since the worker may move to other firms and utilise those skills elsewhere. Hence the onus is entirely on the worker to bear the cost of such training. Completely specific training, in contrast, is of no use at all to other firms. Here the firm is quite likely to meet some or all of the costs of such specific training. Although the firm runs the risk that the trained worker will leave, this risk is far less than with general training since the worker stands to lose by the move as well. In the latter case it is only experience within the company that will enhance the productivity of the worker and this suggests that, as a minimum requirement, experience should be classified into that which occurs before and after engagement with the current employer.

4. The measurement of discrimination

A common approach in most studies of discrimination is to estimate what earnings would have been in the absence of discrimination and compare these with actual earnings. The difference between predicted and actual is the measure of discrimination. Because it measures what is left after other factors have been accounted for, the approach is called the residual method. It is also residual because it might

Tackling discrimination

include other unidentified variables. The crucial factor is, therefore, the estimate of what would have happened without discrimination, i.e. the alternative position. Such a problem is common to many other investigations in economics, e.g. the effects of U.K. membership of the E.E.C., and the effects of mergers on company performance. We cannot control for other factors by laboratory-type experiments and we are forced to use some other method. What alternative assumptions can be made?

The simplest to apply, but most naive, is to assume that female average earnings would be the same as male average earnings in the absence of discrimination. A list of five factors was given above (p. 58) which could lead to differences in average earnings. It is only if all five can be classed as discriminatory that such a procedure is valid. It is our belief, shared by many in the field, that there are other reasons apart from discrimination which would give rise to differences in male and female earnings. Clearly, we must control for differences in productivity which have non-discriminatory causes. At the level of the firm it seems reasonable to take certain features of the labour force as given and outside the control of the employer. In particular, account should be taken of differences in the level of education and any role stereotyping generated by society at large which may result in one sex being less productive than the other in the workplace.

Informed writers on discrimination, therefore, reject the simplistic approach, in favour of some attempt to control for underlying productivity or performance differences. The conventional approach of economists is to estimate an earnings function, as discussed above, and use such a function to predict an alternative wage. One frequently used method is to estimate a common earnings function across the sexes but incorporate an explanatory variable, recording the sex of the employee. This might take the value of 1 if the worker is a male and 0 if female. Such a variable is known as a dummy variable.[15] It allows the intercept of the function (that is the point at which the regression line cuts the vertical axis) to differ whilst assuming the coefficients on the other variables are identical between the sexes. The proposition can be illustrated by a simple example. Assume that the wage is related to a single variable such as experience, and that the relationship can be represented by a straight line. This will be upward sloping if the pay system rewards workers with greater experience by higher pay. In Figure 5.1, two separate lines are drawn

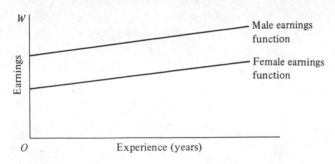

Figure 5.1 Male and female earnings – different intercept

for males and females with that for males being above that for
females. Thus, for any given level of experience, the male wage will
be higher than that for a female. Since the slopes of the lines are
assumed to be the same, the difference between male and female
earnings will be constant for every level of experience. This difference
between the two lines is frequently taken as a measure of discrimination. The use of dummy variables in this way is discussed in
a more technical way in Appendix 5.1. Although it is commonly
used, we consider this method to be potentially misleading. There
seems no good reason for assuming that the slopes of the lines would
be the same if discrimination existed. Indeed there are good grounds
for believing that discriminating employers would assign different
values to the slopes. For instance, they might treat an increase in
the experience of a woman less favourably than a similar increase
for a male. There will also be many more variables than just
experience which influence earnings and there is little justification
for assuming that employers treat all these the same regardless of
the sex of the worker. In Appendix 5.1, the two basic methods of
introducing differences in the slopes are discussed. The one that we
prefer is to estimate two separate equations – one for males and one
for females. Using our simple illustration of only one variable
(experience) the position could look as in Figure 5.2. In this diagram
not only does the male line have a higher intercept but it also has a
steeper slope and thus the difference in earnings gets larger as
experience is greater.

The equations can be estimated by standard linear regression
procedures as discussed in Appendix 5.1, and having done this it is
important to assess whether the male and female equations really

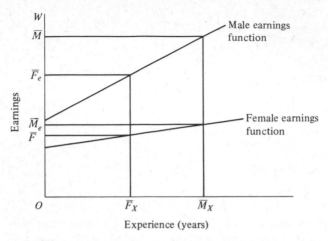

Figure 5.2 Male and female earnings – different slopes and intercept

are different or whether any observed discrepancies could have occurred by chance. If the two equations are shown to be statistically significantly different it is often assumed to represent *a priori* evidence of discrimination. The appropriateness of this working definition will be taken up below. But, accepting it for the moment, it is necessary to consider how the extent of discrimination can be measured.

There are a variety of procedures for the quantification of the discriminatory component but the most generally accepted seems to be that originally proposed by Oaxaca.[16] He suggested two basic alternatives: (i) that men and women would both be paid according to the male equation in the absence of discrimination, or (ii) that they would both be paid according to the female equation.

Again, the technical procedures are more appropriately discussed in the Appendix but the principle can be illustrated using the simple model outlined above and shown in Figure 5.2. Assume that the average female has experience shown by $\bar{F}_X$ whilst the average male has greater experience shown as $\bar{M}_X$. The average female wage would be $\bar{F}$ and the average male wage would be $\bar{M}$. The difference in average wages is, therefore, $\bar{M} - \bar{F}$. But, if the average female was paid the same wage as a male with the same experience she would receive a wage of $\bar{F}_e$. The difference between this estimate of what the average female would earn were she male and the average male wage ($\bar{F}_e - \bar{M}$) represents the fact that the average male has more experience than the average female. On the other hand the difference between this estimated female wage and the actual female average is not accounted for by any difference in experience but because the two equations differ. Such a difference is frequently attributed to discrimination.

The alternative method suggested by Oaxaca is to look at what happens at the average male experience level. In this case the part of the gross difference accounted for by the greater experience of males is $\bar{M}_e - \bar{F}$ and that arising from the difference in the equations is $\bar{M} - \bar{M}_e$. In Figure 5.2 it is clear that this second method yields a higher estimate of the proportion of the gross difference, which is interpreted as discrimination.

Thus we have two alternative measures of discrimination which will give two alternative answers even from the same basic data. Appendix 5.2 discusses in more detail the factors involved in the choice of an actual measure but it is worth pointing out that there are further difficulties which stem from the fact that the true position may not be as simple as that implied in Figure 5.2. Suppose, for example, that, whilst the male relationship has a greater slope than the female, the female has a higher intercept. There would be nothing, in practice, to prevent this occurring. In such a case the two lines would cross as shown in Figure 5.3. At any experience level less than

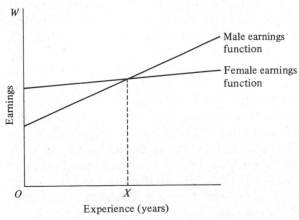

Figure 5.3 Male and female earnings – different slopes and intercepts with crossover

that at the point where the curves cross (*X*) it would appear that there is discrimination in favour of women since they would receive a higher wage than equivalent males. Thus it is apparent that it is not only differences between equations which matter but also the level of the variables that are under consideration. Such a problem is only one of a number involved in interpreting any given measure of discrimination.

5. Problems of interpretation

There are two fundamental requirements if the earnings function approach is to provide a satisfactory assessment of the existence of discrimination: (i) the correct specification of the earnings function; and (ii) that differences between earnings functions can rightly be regarded as evidence of discrimination.

On the first point, since what is left over after differences in characteristics have been controlled for – the residual – is being interpreted as discrimination, it is important that the earnings equations include all variables that are non-discriminatory in nature. As noted above, one of the arguments for concentrating on the analysis of discrimination at the level of the individual firm is that the quality of data may be sufficient to enable one to achieve this and at least some of the sources of error can be minimised.

One of the most important problems concerns the omission of relevant explanatory variables from the earnings function. In econometric terms this can give rise to what is termed 'omitted-variable bias' in that the estimates of the coefficients of the variable that are included may not accurately describe the true relationship. Particular concern arises if the omitted variables are correlated with the included variables. In the standard case it is often fairly simple to determine whether the coefficients are biased upwards or downwards,[17] but where two separate equations are estimated and then used to assess the degree of discrimination, the issue is not so straightforward.[18] The assessment of the direction of bias on the measure of discrimination is not simply a matter of the correlation between the included and excluded variables and the sign of the latter's coefficients. It also depends on the magnitude and sign of the differences between the sexes in the values of the characteristics, both measured and omitted. Thus, high correlation between included and excluded variables does not necessarily imply any serious bias on the discrimination coefficient if the characteristics differ in the 'right' direction and to the 'right' extent. On the other hand, differences in characteristics may serve to reinforce the bias. The sign and magnitude of any bias thus remain unclear and it is in general impossible to say whether the estimated measure of discrimination is likely to be an upper or a lower limit. It therefore becomes important that the earnings function should include all the relevant variables.

But this raises a fundamental problem: what are the relevant variables? The question concerns the validity of including certain variables in estimating discrimination and there are two basic issues involved: (i) different treatment for the same characteristics whatever they might be; and (ii) the reasonableness of the criteria adopted by the firm in determining earnings, hiring or promotion and whether these have the effect of discriminating by sex.

It seems appropriate that the earnings differential should be partitioned into that based on reasonable characteristics and that based on unreasonable characteristics. But on what criteria is this to be done? As noted in Chapter 1, this dilemma is alluded to in the indirect discrimination provisions of the Sex Discrimination Act.

As outlined above, most of the empirical studies of discrimination are based on equations which contain work experience and schooling as major explanatory variables. However, it is not altogether clear that experience and schooling would gain universal support as to their 'reasonableness'. This depends very much on the nature of the job. If the model were extended to include test scores of various kinds, socio-economic background variables etc. it would no longer be apparent that identical treatment of a measured characteristic constitutes non-discriminatory behaviour, since these variables do not necessarily indicate differences in performance. Analysis of decision-taking within the family has suggested that differences in some coefficients within the earnings function are perfectly consistent with non-discriminatory behaviour. The work of Mincer and Polachek[19] would seem to imply that identical coefficients on the experience variables would amount to reverse discrimination since one year's labour-market experience of a woman is likely to embody less investment in human capital than for a man. Correspondingly, different treatment of the same measured characteristics echoed in a different functional relationship does not necessarily amount to discriminatory behaviour if the characteristics are unreasonable in the sense that their measurement is sexually biased.

Most of the studies conducted tend to relate to discrimination which takes place after entry to the labour force or particular employment (post-entry discrimination) and do not control for preconditioning, differential education opportunities etc. (pre-entry discrimination). This, in fact, is the sensible approach when one is examining whether a specific decision-maker (employer) is discriminating against women, since these aspects will be outside his/her control. They are extremely important, however, if one is seeking to estimate the extent of discrimination in the country at large.

A further problem of interpretation relates to the fact that the relationship between the wages received and the characteristics of the individuals reflects observed outcomes. These observed outcomes are the result of the interaction between supply- and demand-side forces. As such it is not possible to be certain that the unexplained earnings differential stems from the demand side of the labour market (employers), and represents discrimination, rather than from the supply side as a result of the tastes and preferences of individual employees influenced by, amongst other things, the division of labour within the household.

Some authors[20] have suggested a further stratification of the data by marital status as a means of overcoming some of these problems. Thus, an important productivity characteristic is motivation to work, which is not easily measured. However, married men are likely to be strongly motivated towards market work, and married women less so, because of the division of labour in the household; hence a step towards controlling for motivation is attained by separating these two groups. Single men and single women might be presumed to have a similar attitude to work and a comparable degree of career orientation as discussed in Chapter 3. Such an argument leads Greenhalgh,[21] amongst others, to suggest that any unexplained differential between single men and women gives the best estimate of discrimination. Further, the effects of family role specialisation can be assessed by comparing the married with the single for men and women separately. Since the argument suggests that the coefficients on all the other productivity-enhancing variables are likely to differ, the appropriate procedure is to estimate separate regressions by sex and by marital status rather than the inclusion of a marital

Table 5.1: *Interpretation of the unexplained earnings differential by sex/marital status group*

Comparator groups	Interpretation
Single women Married women	Family role of wife
Married men Single women	Family role of husband plus discrimination
Married men Single men	Family role of husband
Single men Single women	Discrimination

status dummy in a single equation. The earnings differential can then be de-composed into an explained and an unexplained portion, as discussed above. There are four comparisons to be made and the interpretation of the residual on the basis of the above analysis would be as shown in Table 5.1.

In principle the idea is appealing, but it has to be remembered that marital status is not unalterable. Behaviour of currently single people will be affected by expectations of their future marital status. Further, marital status may not be the important determining factor but rather the presence (or expectation) of children of school age.

It might perhaps also be worth investigating the possibility of estimating separate earnings functions according to whether children are, or are not, present within the household. The fundamental problem is that one is trying to evaluate lifetime behaviour from a cross-section taken at one particular point in time when it is really necessary to examine the marriage decision[22] and its effects on labour-market behaviour in much more depth. Without such an analysis and improved empirical investigation, simple stratification by marital status is open to serious problems of interpretation.

Looking at the analysis of discrimination within individual firms may cause problems of sample size, if a four-way split into married and single, male and female is to be made. This makes it difficult to apply our procedure in very small firms. In addition the records of the firm may not contain any information on the current marital status of the employee. It is of course not too difficult to obtain such information and any employer seeking to carry out an analysis of the type described here is advised to follow this practice.

We have discussed in some detail the problems inherent in any attempt to measure discrimination, even where this is limited to the place of work. Discrimination itself is such a complex phenomenon that it is not surprising that severe difficulties face the conscientious investigator. The earnings-function approach suggested here cannot be taken as decisive evidence of the existence of discrimination. Nevertheless the results, if handled carefully, are illustrative of the magnitudes involved and are an essential first step in getting to grips with the problem. We illustrate the typical application and results of such studies in the following section. The studies undertaken reflect a wide range of circumstances.

6. Empirical studies of sex discrimination in British organisations

The first study of sex discrimination in Britain conducted along the lines discussed above was that of Chiplin and Sloane.[23] It was based on a sample of over 500 workers in a specific occupation within a particular large multiplant organisation. The workers under analysis were a professional group with high educational qualifications. Since the majority of those involved had identical years of schooling, the schooling variable was excluded from the model. The occupation in the firm had two distinct levels – level 1 and level 2 – where level 1 was the sole port of entry for promotion to level 2. The experience of the worker was broken down into three elements: (i) work experience within the company at level 1, (ii) work experience within the company at level 2, (iii) work experience outside the company.

Table 5.2 shows the results of fitting an earnings function containing these experience terms and their squares. The male and female equations are statistically significantly different, and three measures of discrimination are shown namely D_3, D_4 and D_8. (These are defined in Appendix 5.2.) The first suggests that, given their experience characteristics, women would be paid a little less favourably if they were treated as males and does not therefore indicate the existence of discrimination against women. Fitting the males to the female equation (D_4) does show some discrimination and the average (D_8) likewise is positive. However given our preference for using D_3 as the standard as explained in Appendix 5.2 it would appear that the evidence for discrimination in this case is not particularly strong.

Table 5.2: *Equations explaining gross salary of workers in a professional occupation in a large British company*

Variable	Males	Females
Constant	7.82	7.73
Level 1 experience	+0.008	+0.04*
	(0.06)	(6.0)
(Level 1 experience)^2	−0.00004	−0.0009*
	(0.11)	(4.3)
Level 2 experience	+0.125*	+0.15*
	(15.1)	(15.4)
(Level 2 experience)^2	−0.004*	−0.008*
	(10.9)	(10.7)
Outside experience	−0.04**	+0.004
	(2.3)	(0.5)
(Outside experience)^2	+0.002*	−0.0001
	(2.2)	(0.3)
R^2	0.67	0.68

Measures of discrimination (%)

$D_3 = -0.162$; $D_4 = 10.8$; $D_8 = 5.5$ (see Appendix 5.2)

Figures in parentheses are t values

* significant at 1% level

** significant at 5% level

Source: Chiplin and Sloane, 'Personal Characteristics and Sex Differentials in Professional Employment', table 1.

Notes: In the first numerical column, the values of the coefficients (e.g. +0.008 etc.) tell us the size and direction of the relationship between that particular variable and gross salary. If the coefficient has one asterisk, we can be pretty sure that there is a reliable relationship (i.e. we have only a one per cent chance of being wrong). Two asterisks indicate we have a five per cent chance of being wrong. The t statistic measures the significance of each variable, the higher the value the greater the reliability. R^2 (the coefficient of determination) measures the goodness of fit of the equation as a whole and indicates the proportion of the variance in the dependent variable (gross earnings) which can be explained by the included variables. Thus in the male equation we are able to explain 67% of the variance in gross earnings

In the above study no attempt was made to estimate separate equations for married and single males and females. In Table 5.3 we report the results of applying the model to five establishments where this did prove feasible. The establishments were involved in light engineering, finance, the public sector, food processing and clothing. For the financial institution and the public-sector organisation only white-collar employees were considered. The food processing and clothing analyses were limited to manual employees whilst the light-engineering case covered all categories. For two of the organisations, the financial institution and the food-processing factory, no details of the education of the employees were available. In the latter case this was not a problem since the large majority of workers were unskilled. In the former, the sample was limited to those who had entered employment by age 16 in order to try to standardise education level.

Looking at the five organisations it appears overall that service with the firm together with education are the most powerful determinants of pay for all four sex/marital status groups. Service outside the current employer only appears important in the public-sector organisation where it is in any case defined to include service elsewhere in the public sector. The insignificance of outside service, coupled with the significance of internal service, suggests strong internal labour markets in the cases considered. The implied stress on continuity of employment in a given organisation is of some importance for the relative earnings of women since their work experience tends to be discontinuous.

Table 5.4 shows the unexplained earnings differential using measures D_3 and D_4 discussed above.[24] In some cases, notably in the comparisons between single and married women, the adjusted ratio is lower than the actual. This implies that married women receive more favourable treatment relative to single women than their measured relative productivity characteristics would merit and gives rise to the negative bracketed figure.

Using the single-male–single-female comparison as the 'best' indicator of sex discrimination shows that women's relative pay is reduced by some 15 per cent to 16 per cent in the engineering company, 9 per cent in the financial institution and there is little discernible effect in the public-sector department. In all three cases it is possible to reject the hypothesis that the earnings functions are the same. As noted above, such a finding can be used to infer the existence of discrimination.

To put the individual firm studies in context it is possible to compare them with results for Great Britain derived by Greenhalgh using the 1971 and 1975 General Household Surveys.[25] The results of her study are shown in Table 5.5. The two alternative estimates of the expected ratio without discrimination are quite close for most of the comparisons except those between married and single women, indicating that the precise measure used does not make such difference to the result. A further set of calculations was made, using a larger model which included variables for occupation and industry. Greenhalgh reports that in general there was little difference between the two sets of estimates but, as expected, controlling for occupation and industry resulted in slightly greater explained differentials and consequently smaller estimates of discrimination and family effects.

The estimates suggest that sex discrimination of about 10 per cent was operating between adult single men and women, but a slightly lower figure was obtained for younger persons (less than 30 years old). Such an order of magnitude is very similar to that obtaining on average in our studies of individual enterprises. Although still open to problems of interpretation it is encouraging that such similar estimates should be found.

According to the Greenhalgh results, the unexplained differential between single and married women is quite large so that the total labour-market disadvantage of married women *vis-a-vis* single men was about twice that of single women. Married men had a 9 per cent differential over single men. Thus, the overall variation in earnings between husbands and wives with similar characteristics is made up of three roughly equal parts; first, the difference between the earnings of married and single men; second, the difference in earnings between single men and single women; and third, the difference in earnings between single women and married women. Hence marital status is just as important as gender in explaining earnings differences.

7. Conclusions

This chapter has examined in some detail the problems involved in assessing and evaluating the extent of discrimination in earnings

Table 5.3: *Earnings functions for five British organisations*

Dependent variable: log earnings	Male		Female excl. part-time	
	Married	Single	Married	Single
Engineering company				
Constant	7.605	7.767	7.671	7.318
SER	.0557*	.0144	.0330	.0626*
SER²	−.0015*	.0003	−.0004	−.0015*
XSER	.0200	.0397	−.0060	.0127
XSER²	−.0006	−.0021	.0002	−.0007
ED	Dummies*	Dummies*	Dummies*	Dummies*
R^2	.563	.845	.347	.834
Financial institution				
Constant	7.398	7.006	7.239	7.033
SER	.0472*	.1117*	.0619*	.0889*
SER²	−.0005	−.0019*	−.0013*	−.0019*
QUA	.1041	−.0390	—	.1292*
R^2	.515	.966	.761	.905
Public service department				
Constant	8.100	7.614	8.048	7.730
SER	.0231*	.1404*	.0397*	.0690*
SER²	−.0002	−.0043*	−.0011	−.0015*
XSER	.0350*	.0216	−.0036	.0655*
XSER²	−.0010*	.0043	.0002	−.0027*

	Dummies*	Dummies*	Dummies*	Dummies*
ED				
DIP	.1775*	.1098	.0593	.8874*
R^2	.722	.904	.681	.924
Food processing factory				
Constant	3.753		3.711	
SER	.0110*		.0006	
SER^2	−.0004*		.0001	
XSER	.0018		.0040	
$XSER^2$	−.0001		−.0001	
R^2	.209		.071	
Clothing factory				
Constant			7.130	7.065
SER			.0662*	.1105*
SER^2			−.0023*	−.0050*
FAM			.0163	—
BREAK			−.0183	−.0513
ED			.4108*	−.0536
REP			−.0111	−.0525
R^2			.286	.312

* denotes significance at the 5% level (in the case of the education dummies* means at least one of the dummies is significant) where each dummy represents a particular level of education e.g. ordinary grade school leaving certificate, higher or advanced grade, degree etc.

Table 5.4: *Earnings ratio under various productivity assumptions by sex/marital status group – 5 establishments*

	Single female	Single male	Married male	Married male
	Married female	Single female	Single male	Married female
Engineering company				
Actual	1.11	1.15	1.16	1.47
Adjusted using function of:				
numerator group[a]	1.23 (−0.11)	0.96 (0.16)	1.04 (0.10)	1.22 (0.17)
denominator group[b]	1.10 (0.01)	0.98 (0.15)	0.97 (0.17)	1.08 (0.27)
Financial institution				
Actual	1.35	1.69	1.79	2.22
Adjusted using function of:				
numerator group[a]	1.03 (0.24)	1.54 (0.09)	1.54 (0.14)	2.0 (0.10)
denominator group[b]	1.10 (0.19)	1.54 (0.09)	1.19 (0.33)	1.20 (0.46)
Public sector department				
Actual	1.08	1.03	1.96	2.17
Adjusted using function of:				
numerator group[a]	1.37 (−0.32)	1.01 (0.02)	1.28 (0.22)	1.32 (0.39)
denominator group[b]	1.09 (−0.01)	1.05 (−0.02)	1.30 (0.21)	1.52 (0.30)

Food processing factory

Actual   1.05

Adjusted using function of:

  numerator group[a]   1.02 (0.03)

Clothing factory

Actual   0.90

Adjusted using function of:

  numerator group[a]   0.90 (0.00)

  denominator group[b]   0.91 (−0.01)

[a] figures in parentheses show calculation of discrimination coefficient D_3 (equation 5.3).

[b] figures in parentheses show calculation of discrimination coefficient D_4 (equation 5.4)

Source: Adapted from Siebert and Sloane, 'The Measurement of Sex and Marital Status Discrimination at the Workplace', Table 2

Table 5.5: *Estimated effects of market discrimination and family role specialisation in Great Britain*

Year	Groups for comparison	Raw differential R	Explained differential[a]		Unexplained differential[b] (%)			Possible interpretation of unexplained differential.
			E_1	E_2	D_3	D_4	D_8	
1971	Single women / Married women	1.452	1.320	1.517	−4.48	9.09	2.5	Family role (wife)
1971	Married men / Single women	1.354	0.867	0.914	32.5	36.0	34.3	Family role (husband) plus discrimination
1975	Single women / Married women	1.418	1.295	1.189	16.2	8.7	12.5	Family role (wife)
1975	Married men / Single women	1.141	0.899	0.935	18.1	21.2	19.6	Family role (husband) plus discrimination
1975	Married men / Single men	1.108	1.005	0.991	10.6	9.3	9.9	Family role (husband)
1975	Single men / Single women	1.029	0.935	0.913	11.3	9.1	10.2	Discrimination
1975	Single men <30 / Single women <30	1.156	1.063	1.064	8.0	8.0	8.0	Discrimination

[a] E_1 and E_2 are the alternative estimated ratios using the coefficients of the denominator group and numerator groups respectively.

[b] $D_3 = (R - E_2)/R$; $D_4 = (R - E_1)/R$; $D_8 = [R - (E_1 \cdot E_2)^{1/2}]/R$

Source: Adapted from C. Greenhalgh, 'Male–Female Wage Differentials in Great Britain', Table 9.

occurring at the place of work. It has been argued that there is no simple solution but, as a minimum, account must be taken of differences in performance-related characteristics which are not under the influence of the particular employer. The use of simple statistics such as the difference in average earnings between male and female workers is a potentially misleading procedure.

We have argued that the most sensible approach is to estimate equations relating the relevant characteristics of workers to their earnings, although the determination of the relevant characteristics is not itself an easy task. Nevertheless it is an important first step by which an organisation can assess the effects of its policies. We have illustrated the approach with a number of examples drawn from British organisations. Although it is dangerous to generalise from a limited number of observations, additional evidence from a national study would tend to support the conclusion that discrimination appears to be about 10 per cent. Such a figure indicates that sex discrimination is roughly one quarter of the crude earnings differential, which demonstrates the importance of controlling for other (performance-related) factors.

APPENDIX 5.1

The use of dummy variables in the estimation of discrimination

Taking the simple case illustrated in Figure 5.1 of one explanatory variable the relevant regression equation would be:

$$\ln W = a + bX + cD + u$$

Where W is the wage rate
X is experience
$D = 1$ if male; 0 if female
u is the error term.

The slopes of the two lines in Figure 5.1 are the same and measured by the coefficient b. The difference between the two lines is given by the value of the coefficient, c, on the dummy variable. In the case illustrated $c > 0$.

Differences in coefficients can be easily introduced and tested in two basic ways: (i) introduce interaction terms between the sex dummy variable and the other variables; or (ii) estimate separate equations for males and females.

In terms of the simple illustration in the former case the equation would be:

$$\ln W = a + bX + cD + d(D.X) + U$$

where U is the error term and $D.X$ is the experience variable multiplied by the dummy. The coefficient d represents the difference between the slopes and its significance can be tested by the usual method (t test). One problem with this approach is the assumption that the variance of the error term is the same for both males and females. There is no *a priori* reason to expect this to be the case and the assumption can be removed by the second method, i.e. the estimation of two separate equations. Thus we have:

$$\ln Wm = am + bmX + Um$$

and

$$\ln Wf = af + bfX + Uf$$

where m represents males and f females and there are independent intercepts, coefficients and error terms for the two sectors. This is the case illustrated by Figure 5.2. The Chow test is the standard statistical procedure to ascertain whether some or all of the coefficients are significantly different in the two cases.[26] That is, any observed difference is not so small that it could have occurred through chance.

APPENDIX 5.2

Alternative measures of discrimination

As noted in the text, there are two broad alternatives to the measurement of discrimination on the basis of earnings functions: either female characteristics are fitted to the estimated male equation or male characteristics are fitted to the female equation. In the former case, estimated mean female wage ($\bar{F}_e$) is given by:

$$\bar{F}_e = f_m(\bar{j}_i F)$$

where f_m represents the male wage equation and $\bar{j}_i F$ is a vector of the mean levels of characteristics of the females. In this case the difference between the actual male average wage ($\bar{M}$) and the actual female average wage ($\bar{F}$) can be de-composed as follows:

$$\bar{M} - \bar{F}_e = \text{the difference in the mean wage attributable to}$$

differences in the mean value of characteristics;

$\bar{F}_e - \bar{F} =$ the residual difference not accounted for by

differences in the average value of characteristics, which is generally ascribed to discrimination.

The alternative is to estimate the male average wage $(\bar{M}_e)$ by

$$\bar{M}_e = f_w(\bar{J}_i M)$$

where f_w is the female wage equation which is evaluated at the mean values of the male characteristics. Here $\bar{M} - \bar{M}_e$ is the residual attributed to discrimination and $\bar{M}_e - \bar{F}$ is the difference in the average wage due to differences in the average levels of characteristics. Hence using this method one can estimate the proportion of the gross difference which is explained by differences in characteristics and there are two possible extreme answers, i.e.

(1) That derived from using the male equation to estimate the average female wage in the absence of discrimination $(\bar{F}_e)$. The residual as a proportion of the total difference is therefore:

$$D_1 = \frac{\bar{F}_e - \bar{F}}{\bar{M} - \bar{F}} = \frac{\bar{F}_e/\bar{F} - 1}{\bar{M}/\bar{F} - 1} \tag{5.1}$$

(2) That derived from using the female equation to estimate the average male wage in the absence of discrimination $(\bar{M}_e)$. The residual as a proportion of the total difference is therefore:

$$D_2 = \frac{\bar{M} - \bar{M}_e}{\bar{M} - \bar{F}} = \frac{1 - \bar{M}_e/\bar{M}}{1 - \bar{F}/\bar{M}} \tag{5.2}$$

An alternative using the same basic information is to examine the ratio of the male to female wage. The expected ratio in the absence of discrimination can be calculated either as $\dfrac{\bar{M}}{\bar{F}_e}$ or as $\dfrac{\bar{M}_e}{\bar{F}}$ using the actual ratio as the denominator. Thus

$$D_3 = \frac{\bar{M}/\bar{F} - \bar{M}/\bar{F}_e}{\bar{M}/\bar{F}} = 1 - \frac{\bar{M}/\bar{F}_e}{\bar{M}/\bar{F}} \tag{5.3}$$

or

$$D_4 = \frac{\bar{M}/\bar{F} - \bar{M}_e/\bar{F}}{\bar{M}/\bar{F}} = 1 - \frac{\bar{M}_e/\bar{F}}{\bar{M}/\bar{F}} \tag{5.4}$$

D_3 and D_4 are closely related to Becker's measure of the generalised market discrimination coefficient which he defined as[27]

$$\text{MDC} = \left(\frac{\bar{M}}{\bar{F}}\right) - \left(\frac{\bar{M}}{\bar{F}}\right)^0$$

where the first term is the actual wage ratio and the second is that which would occur in the absence of discrimination. The measures are therefore simply the discrimination coefficients divided by the actual ratio. Clearly an alternative denominator would be the expected wage ratio in which case we have two further possible measures:

$$D_5 = \frac{\bar{M}/\bar{F} - \bar{M}/\bar{F}_e}{\bar{M}/\bar{F}_e} = \frac{\bar{M}/\bar{F}}{\bar{M}/\bar{F}_e} - 1 \qquad (5.5)$$

and

$$D_6 = \frac{\bar{M}/\bar{F} - \bar{M}_e/\bar{F}}{\bar{M}_e/\bar{F}} = \frac{\bar{M}/\bar{F}}{\bar{M}_e/\bar{F}} - 1 \qquad (5.6)$$

The choice between the denominators is essentially arbitrary. The first gives a measure of the proportion of relative wages unexplained whereas the second gives the proportion by which the actual exceeds the expected. For each set of measures there is a choice between estimating what the typical female would receive in the absence of discrimination and estimating what the typical male would be paid. Although there is no obvious base, assigning the female characteristics to the male equation to calculate $\bar{F}_e$ may be regarded as being equivalent to using a base-weighted (Laspeyres) price index and assigning the male characteristics to the female equation to calculate $\bar{M}_e$ as equivalent to a current-weighted (Paasche) price index. The importance of the difference in the average value of characteristics is conversely evaluated in terms of a current-weighted quantity index in the former case and a base-weighted quantity index in the latter.

Let p_f stand for the price paid for units of characteristics in the female equation; p_m for the price paid for units of characteristics in the male equation; and q_m and q_f for the average quantities of characteristics possessed by males and females respectively. Assigning female characteristics to the male equation produces the following estimate of the contribution of different 'prices':

$$\frac{\Sigma p_m q_f}{\Sigma p_f q_f} = \text{base-weighted price index} \qquad (5.7)$$

or

$$\bar{F}_e = \frac{\Sigma p_m q_f}{\Sigma p_f q_f} \cdot \Sigma p_f q_f = \Sigma p_m q_f \tag{5.8}$$

Alternatively, assigning male characteristics to the female equation yields:

$$\frac{\Sigma p_m q_m}{\Sigma p_f q_m} = \text{current-weighted price index} \tag{5.9}$$

or

$$\bar{M}_e = \left(\frac{\Sigma p_m q_m}{\Sigma p_f q_m} \cdot \frac{1}{\Sigma p_m q_m} \right)^{-1} = p_f q_m \tag{5.10}$$

Since one is seeking to explain the whole of the differential in earnings, the corresponding indexes for the quantities of characteristics are:

$$\frac{\Sigma p_m q_m}{\Sigma p_m q_f} = \text{current-weighted quantity index} \tag{5.11}$$

or

$$\frac{\Sigma p_f q_m}{\Sigma p_f q_f} = \text{base-weighted quantity index} \tag{5.12}$$

These and other methods for the measurement of discrimination have been criticised by Boulet and Rowley.[28] The main point of their criticism is that any measure should show that e.g. the measure of discrimination against one sex is equal to the measure of discrimination in favour of the other sex. The above procedures do not satisfy the criterion and Boulet and Rowley themselves suggest no procedure for meeting the problem. Although as a general principle their criticism has some validity it is by no means clear that the property of symmetry is desirable in the particular context of discrimination. If there is no favouritism towards men but discrimination against women then the theory suggests that men would be paid their marginal product but women would be paid less.[29] In this case removal of discrimination would imply that women would be paid according to the male function and the approach implied in 5.8 would be appropriate. If there is favouritism towards men they would receive more than their marginal product and the composite function arising after the removal of both discrimination and favouritism would lie somewhere between the existing male and female functions. Given the numerical superiority of males in the working population it seems likely that this would be closer to the male rather than the female function and 5.8 is again the most suitable. As Masters has noted the essence of discrimination is that it is asymmetric.[30]

If it is felt desirable to have a single estimate of the wage or ratio which would occur without discrimination it is possible to take some average of the alternative estimates. For instance, measures D_3 and D_4 (equations 5.3 and 5.4) could be combined to produce a single measure by taking the arithmetic average of the two estimated ratios:

$$D_7 = \frac{\dfrac{\bar{M}}{\bar{F}} - \dfrac{1}{2}\left(\dfrac{\bar{M}}{\bar{F}_e} + \dfrac{\bar{M}_e}{\bar{F}}\right)}{\bar{M}/\bar{F}} \tag{5.13}$$

In her work with U.K. data Greenhalgh uses essentially this approach. An alternative, and one which fits in well with the index number analysis discussed earlier, would be to take the geometric rather than the arithmetic mean of the ratios, i.e.:

$$D_8 = \frac{\dfrac{\bar{M}}{\bar{F}} - \left(\dfrac{\bar{M}}{\bar{F}_e} \cdot \dfrac{\bar{M}_e}{\bar{F}}\right)^{1/2}}{\bar{M}/\bar{F}} \tag{5.14}$$

The square root term is equivalent to a Fisher's Ideal Index[32] obtained from the two alternative quantity indexes:

$$\left(\frac{\bar{M}}{\bar{F}_e} \cdot \frac{\bar{M}_e}{\bar{F}}\right)^{1/2} = \left(\frac{p_m q_m}{p_f q_m} \cdot \frac{p_m q_f}{p_f q_f}\right)^{1/2} \tag{5.15}$$

As noted above, however, the actual single function that would be established in a non-discriminatory market is unclear. Our preference remains with those estimates which assign the female characteristics to the male equation i.e. D_1, D_2 or D_5. There does not seem any strong argument in favour of some averaging process as in D_7 or D_8.

6
The recruitment of labour

1. Introduction

We have already focussed on the question of entry into the establishment or firm in section 3(a) of Chapter 4. This is particularly important for equality of opportunity as there is reason to believe that increasing firm size, allied to capital intensity and technological change, may lead to the development of internal labour markets with limited ports of entry. That is, firms may hire workers only at the lower levels of broad occupational classifications, and train their own workers for higher-level jobs through promotion from within. Thus, groups of workers who are unable to gain entry to the firm at the lower levels may lose any possibility of employment in that firm in the future. It is important to understand therefore the process of filling jobs, including such factors as the propensity to use gender as a cheap screening device, the importance of relevant information, or the lack of it, for determining selection, and the significance of self-selection by particular groups, such as women, in restricting job choice. Knowledge of these factors should provide some guide to how far these processes are amenable to change through legislation or other means.

There are several stages to the hiring process. In terms of recruitment the first step is to prepare a job description and, since it is often difficult to distinguish between the job role and its occupant, this specification will draw heavily on the attributes of past job-holders. Second, as noted in Chapter 4, there are several means of attracting applicants, including informal channels, press advertisements and the public-employment services; and the varied use of any of these channels may affect the probability of attracting members of a particular sex. In terms of selection the major problem is that information about performance potential is not directly observable until an individual has actually taken up a post. Here neo-classical economic theory has emphasised the importance of market imperfections, such as lack of information, in determining both employee selection by the employer and job choice by the employee. The net result of this situation may be that gender is used as a cheap screening device; that is, decisions are based upon group performance rather than the expected performance of a particular applicant. In this respect one may usefully distinguish between indices (such as race, sex and age) which cannot be altered by the individual concerned and signals (such as education) which can be so changed.[1] On the employer side the potential gain from isolating those females whose performance compares favourably with that of males would have to be compared with the costs of obtaining this information. Prior assessment may alter as a result of experience gained from employing females in what were formerly male-dominated jobs, which might happen with the elimination of discrimination against women. Yet it remains a possibility that employers may react to the outlawing of gender as a cheap screening device merely by substituting another form which is not based upon gender and therefore might be permissible. On the employee side, on the other hand, it should be recognised that females may not apply for certain jobs because the latter require, or reward, attributes possessed almost exclusively by male employees (e.g. wage structures geared to length of service), and these supply-side differences are likely to remain important elements in the segregation of jobs.

In order to cast light on some of these issues we carried out studies of hiring practices in local labour markets in the East Midlands and the West of Scotland and an analysis of selection for entry into a university economics department. In the first two studies we carried out an analysis of Employment Services Agency job vacancy data for one Job Centre in each of two areas (East Midlands and West of Scotland). This was prior to the introduction of the Sex Discrimination Act in 1975, and at that time vacancies were differentiated according to gender, a practice that has ceased since the introduction of the legislation. These data provide information on initial perceptions by management of job requirements. In the West of Scotland study the vacancy data were also analysed in the six months following the introduction of the legislation to ascertain whether any significant changes had occurred relating to the segregation of the sexes. This study, outlined below, establishes that the main overlap area where employers were apparently prepared to accept applications from members of either sex was the clerical and related occupational category. In order to investigate this further, firms that had advertised vacancies in this occupational group in the local press were approached immediately after the filling of the job vacancy. This was in order for us to determine relevant factors in the hiring decision. There were 78 interviews held in the East Midlands and 74 in the West of Scotland.[2] The third study examines access to education, an important factor in the relative job position as indicated in Chapter 3. We asked whether, once women have decided to apply for a particular course of study at a U.K. university, there is any evidence that their application is given discriminatory treatment. That is, do women (or men) have a lower probability of receiving an offer of a place for given characteristics? The focus here is thus on the offer of a post or place rather than the numbers actually on a course, allowing for the fact that sometimes offers will be rejected by the applicant. Though this study concerns entry to a particular course of study, the methodology is also applicable to the question of entry to a particular job in the labour market.

2. Employment Services Agency vacancy study

The source of data in the East Midlands was the record of vacancies notified to the relevant district office of the Employment Services Agency (E.S.A.) between 1 May 1974 and 31 October 1974 inclusive. The sample for this period consisted of 5,009 vacancies, comprising all vacancies notified to the Commercial section, all vacancies notified to the women's industrial section and a one-in-three random sample of vacancies notified to the men's industrial section. The comparable data for the West of Scotland consisted of all vacancies notified to the Job Centre over the six months ending in September 1975 (1,799 vacancies). In addition a separate analysis was conducted of West of Scotland vacancy cards over the period of six months prior to the enactment of the Sex Discrimination Act on 29 December 1975 and the first six months subsequent to it.[3] A random sample of one in two cards was taken and this provided a total of 1,315 observations (592 being in the pre-Act period and 723 in the post-Act period). It should be noted that in many cases a single specification applied to several vacancies. Since such specifications were weighted by the number of vacancies represented, the sample figures are of total vacancies notified rather than the smaller number of job specifications. The data are also only as complete and reliable as the E.S.A. record card for that vacancy allows. For example, the omission of mention of training does not necessarily imply that none is offered or provided, merely that this was not mentioned when the vacancy was notified.

For purposes of comparison, percentage figures for each major occupational group, specified as male, female or mixed according to employer preferences over a period of six months, ending in October 1974 in the case of the East Midlands and September 1975 in the case of the West of Scotland, are contained in Table 6.1.[4] At this level of aggregation it can be seen that there is a marked degree of occupational segregation by sex; with construction, mining, transport-operating and related occupations, and materials-processing and repairing being male-dominated occupations, and clerical and selling being female-dominated. Overall, in only a small minority of cases do employers specify job vacancies as being open to either sex, which suggests that there is a significant amount of segregation even within these occupational groups. It also appears that female vacancies are concentrated in fewer occupations than are male. The degree of segregation is more marked in the West of Scotland than in the East Midlands both in terms of the 'maleness' and 'femaleness' of the occupational groups and in terms of the proportion of vacancies which are open to either sex. It is not possible to ascertain from a study of this nature, however, how far this is a function of differences in industrial structure, in the tightness of the labour market or in attitudes to female employment. However, the very much larger 'mixed' category in Nottingham suggests the situation can vary from one area to another.

A more detailed breakdown by 18 major occupational groups is provided for the West of Scotland Job Centre in Table 6.2. Only 1.9 per cent of vacancies fall within the mixed sex category and, even in occupations where both sexes are recruited in considerable numbers, very few fall within this category. Thus, although the major group X is a catch-all category it does contain 77 unskilled cleaners and yet in only 11 cases were jobs advertised as being open to both sexes. It is difficult to believe that the nature of the job determined such differences, though we must not neglect the possibility that, in addition to employer or union preferences, the willingness of females to offer themselves for certain jobs could be a contributory factor.

It is useful to examine the features of the job vacancies according

Table 6.1: *Vacancies notified by occupation and sex for West of Scotland – 6 months ending September 1975 – and East Midlands – 6 months ending October 1974*

		Percentage of occupational category, specified as					
		Male		Female		Either sex	
		%		%		%	
C.O.D.O.T.	Major group	W. Scot.	E. Mid.	W. Scot.	E. Mid.	W. Scot.	E. Mid.
II–V	Professional and related	55.5	60.5	40.7	18.4	3.7	21.0
I, VI	Managerial and related	60.0	64.0	40.0	20.0	0.0	16.0
VII	Clerical	13.8	10.9	81.7	62.4	4.5	26.7
VIII	Selling	11.1	27.7	83.3	59.9	5.6	12.5
IX, X	Catering, cleaning and other services	31.5	45.7	64.7	52.9	3.7	1.4
XII–XIV	Materials processing and repairing (incl. foremen)	74.4	81.7	25.5	18.2	0.1	0.1
XV	Painting, rep. assembly, packaging and related	61.5	63.4	30.7	36.5	7.7	0.1
XVI	Construction, mining	100.0	100.0	0.0	0.0	0.0	0.0
XVII	Transport-operating and related	98.2	99.5	1.8	0.5	0.0	0.0
XVIII, XI	Misc. incl. agriculture	46.8	95.1	52.6	4.9	0.6	0.0

Note: C.O.D.O.T. is the Classification of Occupations and Directory of Occupational Titles used in government statistics

Table 6.2: *Vacancies notified at West of Scotland Job Centre – 6 months ending September* 1975

C.O.D.O.T.	Major group	Male	Female	Either sex	Total
I	Managerial occupations (general management)	0	0	0	0
II	Professional and related supporting management and admin.	0	0	0	0
III	Professional and related in education, welfare and health	1	9	0	10
IV	Literary, artistic and sports	3	1	1	5
V	Professional and related in science, engineering and technology	11	0	0	11
VI	Managerial excl. general management	3	2	0	5
VII	Clerical and related	34	201	11	246
VIII	Selling occupations	12	90	6	108
IX	Security and protective service occupations	15	1	0	16
X	Catering, cleaning, hairdressing and personal service	78	190[a]	11	279
XI	Farming, fishing and related	3	0	0	3
XII	Materials processing occupations excl. metal (incl. foremen)	16	46	0	62
XIII	Making and repairing occupations excl. metal (incl. foremen)	26	16	0	42
XIV	Processing, making and repairing occupations, metal and electrical (incl. foremen)	174	12	0	186
XV	Painting, repetitive assembly, product inspecting, packaging and related	16	8	2	26
XVI	Construction, mining and related N.E.S.	59[b]	0	0	59
XVII	Transport-operating, materials moving, storing and related	229[c]	3	1	233
XVIII	Miscellaneous occupations	236[d]	269[d]	3	508
Total		916	848	35	1799

[a] Includes 77 cleaners
[b] Mainly other construction
[c] Mainly light vehicle drivers
[d] Of whom 235 (266) males (females) were general labourers

to whether employers have a preference for one sex or the other and also whether the attributes they search for in potential appointees differ according to sex.

The most obvious feature is the level of pay. In general, rates of pay attaching to those vacancies tend to be relatively low in relation to current average earnings, which confirms other findings that vacancies notified to the public-employment service tend to be concentrated in the less-skilled groups. In general, employers specify the pay attaching to a particular vacancy, whether minimum, average or a pay scale. In both the East Midlands and the West of Scotland, the pay levels quoted are significantly higher where a preference for males is specified than where the preference is for females. Thus, where a single earnings figure is provided, the mean for women is only 79 per cent of that of men in the East Midlands. In the West of Scotland the comparable figure was 65 per cent prior to the Act and 68 per cent post-Act.

In the large majority of cases employers specify the basic length of working week that the vacancy entails. Part-time work is largely the prerogative of females in both labour markets. Not unexpectedly the average length of working week is slightly above average for those vacancies for which males were sent for interview and slightly below average for females. Overtime working is frequently specified for the male group, but rarely for females. One difference between the two markets is that in the East Midlands the vacancy specifies shift-work in nearly 18 per cent of male vacancies as opposed to less than one per cent of female, whilst, in the West of Scotland, shift-work and inconvenient hours (defined as hours outside the conventional times of 8.00 a.m. to 5.00 p.m.) taken together are more likely to be specified in the female vacancies.

Age is apparently specified by employers in a minority of cases and it is more common to specify a minimum than a maximum age regardless of sex and less frequent still to specify an actual age range. There is a preference for younger rather than older employees regardless of sex. Age discrimination could serve as a proxy for sex discrimination on account of the fact that the female age distribution is significantly different from that of males in the labour force as a whole. There is in fact some tendency for age to be specified more often in those age ranges in which females are more frequently non-participants in the labour force as a consequence of family commitments, but the similarities between the sexes are perhaps more striking than the differences.

In 99 per cent of both male and female vacancies and 83 per cent of those vacancies where there was no sex preference in the East Midlands no qualifications were demanded, which reflected the relatively low mean skill level of the vacancies announced. In approximately 75 per cent of the West of Scotland's vacancies no qualifications were demanded and, where they were, there was a clear segregation in so far as typing was required for a substantial minority of 'female' vacancies and apprenticeship for a substantial minority of 'male' vacancies. This indicates the importance of signals in determining sex differences in occupational composition, since men generally do not have typing diplomas and women do not have apprenticeships.[5]

About 25 per cent of both male and female vacancies in the East Midlands specified an experience requirement, but in the West of Scotland this was true of no less than 66 per cent of the vacancies, with a tendency for such a specification to be more frequent where females were required and perhaps reflecting the easier labour market there. Females as a group will, of course, be put at a disadvantage where experience is a criterion in employers' hiring specifications, particularly in so far as this reflects a preference for more experience, rather than less, and not simply a requirement for some experience. Perhaps surprisingly, training tends to be offered by employers in both labour markets slightly more often for female than for male vacancies and to some extent this may offset the disadvantage experienced by women in relation to experience.

The above personal characteristics are job-related to varying degrees. Employers may, however, specify other personal characteristics which are more closely related to the personality of the individual applicant and which in part may be more directly gender related. Such personal characteristics provide a way of expressing a preference for a particular sex without direct reference to gender as such, since certain characteristics are more likely to be associated with males (e.g. physical strength or possession of a driving licence), and others with females (e.g. manual dexterity or attractive appearance).

The West of Scotland data were sufficiently detailed to enable an analysis to be made of this issue. The most striking feature of those personal characteristics specified as desirable to employers contained in Table 6.3 is the fact that significantly fewer characteristics are recorded in the post-Act period than previously. It is not clear whether this reflects changed recording procedures on the part of the E.S.A. or employers feeling that detailed specification was not necessary in an easier labour market or fearing to infringe the new legislation.

For males the most frequently specified attributes are health and dependability, whilst appearance and dependability are most frequently referred to for females. The most significant differences between the sexes occur in the cases of appearance and ownership of a driving licence. Appearance hardly seems likely to be directly related to performance other than in occupations where contact with the public is important and the frequency of its occurrence is therefore higher than one might expect. The fact that the percentage of times it is specified for females has fallen in the post-Act period[6] does not suggest that its major function is to denote the desired sex of the appointee. Attributes which might be felt to be closely related to productivity in certain tasks such as physique, absence of family commitments and dexterity are notable for their comparative absence. Health could be related to productivity either through its direct effect on performance or indirectly through its effect on absence from work, but the frequency with which it is specified again might imply that the E.S.A. has a large proportion of job applicants who are difficult to employ.

A regression analysis was conducted (reported in full in Appendix 6.1) in order to find out what characteristics tend to determine the sex of the appointee. From this analysis it appears that age, overtime, apprenticeship, physique, a requirement for special tasks, health and a driving licence are male appointee characteristics and experience, typing, appearance and dexterity are female appointee characteristics.

The West of Scotland data also allow us to examine whether the introduction of the legislation made any difference in the short run to the specifications of the employers regarding vacancies and the response of the employment service. In fact the occupational distribution of women sent for interview appears to be more concentrated after the introduction of the legislation than it was previously. If we take the three occupations in which the greatest number of observations occur, separately for men and women, we find that 63.6 per cent of males were concentrated in three occupations pre-Act and 59.0 per cent post-Act, whilst the corresponding figures for females were 85.6 per cent and 89.0 per cent.

Table 6.3: *Personal characteristics coded by sex of person sent for interview by the West of Scotland Job Centre*

| | Pre-Act[a] | | | | | | | | Post-Act[a] | | | | | | | |
| | Male | | Female | | Mixed | | Total | | Male | | Female | | Mixed | | Total | |
Characteristics	No.	%	No.	%	No.	%	No.	%	No.	%	No.	%	No.	%	No.	%
Physique																
not specified	262		220		31		576		248		219		124		713	
specified	10	3.7	2	0.9	2	6.1	16	2.7	8	3.1	0	0.0	0	0.0	10	1.4
Special tasks																
not specified	201		190		28		478		193		206		107		618	
specified	71	26.1	32	14.4	5	15.2	114	19.3	63	24.6	13	5.9	17	13.7	105	14.5
Appearance																
Not specified	192		53		11		290		214		89		42		421	
specified	80	29.4	169	76.1	22	65.6	302	51.0	42	16.4	130	59.4	82	66.1	302	41.8
Family ties																
not specified	271		215		33		583		254		213		120		707	
specified	1	0.4	7	3.2	0	0.0	9	1.5	2	0.8	6	2.7	4	3.2	16	2.2
Health																
not specified	67		102		15		207		166		194		100		568	
specified	205	75.4	120	54.1	18	54.5	385	65.0	90	35.2	25	11.4	24	19.4	155	21.4

Dependability								
not specified	69	64	17	173	167	143	80	475
specified	203 74.6	158 71.2	16 48.5	419 70.8	89 34.8	76 34.7	44 35.5	248 34.3
Dexterity								
not specified	272	220	33	590	256	217	124	721
specified	0 0.0	2 0.9	0 0.0	2 0.3	0 0.0	2 0.9	0 0.0	2 0.3
Social interaction								
not specified	212	180	27	474	242	206	109	676
specified	60 22.1	42 18.9	6 18.2	118 19.9	14 5.5	13 5.9	15 12.1	47 6.5
Driving licence								
not specified	195	221	32	503	183	218	114	625
specified	77 28.3	1 0.5	1 3.0	89 15.0	73 28.5	1 0.5	10 8.1	98 13.6

[a] Pre-Act refers to the period of six months prior to the implementation of the Sex Discrimination Act and Post-Act to the period of six months following its implementation

The latter result is even more marked when the analysis is conducted in terms of appointees, the figures for females being 83.3 per cent pre-Act and 91.3 per cent post-Act. Against this must be set the fact that the mixed group has increased in size. Also, pre-Act, where gender was specified, the E.S.A. sent mixed applicants in 6.3 per cent of cases, but post-Act this figure rose to 20.9 per cent.[7] This would suggest that the E.S.A. had made some attempt to operate in the spirit of the legislation. Yet the outcome was not very different in terms of sex of appointee and there is some indication that jobs in the mixed category possess attributes which are closer to those of female rather than male jobs. Thus the three occupational groups in which both sexes were sent for interview most frequently post-Act were those with the largest number of female applicants. Therefore, it appears that there was a tendency to send males to previously female-dominated jobs rather than to send females to previously male-dominated jobs. This could be a reflection of declining employment opportunities for males.

As far as the employers' response is concerned it is worth noting that the tendency to specify earnings was higher in the post-Act period for both sexes. Earnings could act as a signal regarding the sex normally recruited to a particular job, high earnings signifying male jobs and low earnings female jobs. Further, there was a significant increase in the percentage of vacancies offering overtime in the male category (44 per cent of cases in the post-Act period compared with 28 per cent earlier), despite the fact that the labour market was slacker in the later period with the length of vacancy duration shortening. Again, this raises the possibility that employers are using overtime as a signal to attract male employees, whilst at the same time deterring females from offering themselves for employment.

One can make general observations about these results. First, we were able to consider only a period of 6 months after the legislation took effect and one should not expect radical changes to occur in the short run. Second, the general impression formed is that hiring is a relatively informal, unscientific procedure (though it should be borne in mind that there are few skilled jobs in this sample) and this suggests there may be problems in identifying cases of unfair treatment of women as far as the Sex Discrimination Act is concerned. On the other hand it means also that the effect of the legislation in overriding employer judgements on hiring standards will not necessarily provoke inefficiency and be cost-increasing. Whilst, for instance, employers may not put a preference for males over females into general effect, on account of the lower absenteeism of the former, this may be compensated for by the fact that present practices may not be wholly efficient either. This could have far-reaching policy implications were these findings to hold more generally.

More specific findings are the high degree of occupational division of labour by gender in the two labour markets, which is more marked in the slacker of them, and the fact that occupations have become more concentrated since the legislation in the West of Scotland, where such data are available. In part this may have been influenced by declining employment opportunities, particularly for males, which have been reflected in shorter vacancy periods, slightly lower pay offers, more temporary jobs and less training. The fact that 'female' jobs, in general, are low-paying and without prospects of promotion is also consistent with the dual-labour-market hypothesis. In the short run at least there is little evidence that the legislation has improved significantly the position of women in this particular labour market.

3. Interview surveys of advertised clerical vacancies

Clerical and related occupations formed the main occupational group in which there was an overlap of the sexes in job recruitment, and so we undertook a further survey of such jobs advertised in the local press relevant to the areas served by each Job Centre in the East Midlands and the West of Scotland. In the former case all 78 interviews were carried out before 29 December 1975 – when the Sex Discrimination Act came into force – but in the latter case the 74 interviews were carried out between October 1975 and June 1976, and here 26 vacancies were advertised after the implementation of the Act.

Since the purpose of the survey was to focus on sex discrimination in hiring, the sample was designed to comprise male/female 'overlap' jobs, and therefore certain clerical occupations considered to be strongly stereotyped by sex were excluded. Hence within the major clerical group VII 'clerical and related occupations' the minor group 'shorthand typewriting and related secretarial occupations' was excluded.

The sample was thus taken from advertisements for vacancies for clerical occupations in the local evening papers over the above-mentioned periods. A record was kept of all such vacancies classified into three groups: male specified, female specified, and sex unspecified. For every date considered the following procedure was adopted with each newspaper:

(i) A count was taken of all advertisements satisfying the above criteria: this was recorded separately for 'male', 'female' and 'unspecified' advertisements.

(ii) A random sample was selected. This was not a precise proportion of all vacancies
    (a) because of the structuring of the sample
    (b) because the procedure adopted precluded the selection of advertisements giving only a telephone number or box number.

(iii) An introductory letter was sent to each employer in the sample giving the 'credentials' of the project.

(iv) Approximately one week later telephone contact was established with the employer and, where co-operation was forthcoming, an interview was arranged with the person responsible for the recruitment decision, after that decision had been made.

(v) Interviews were conducted and recorded.

To the extent that women are discriminated against in the labour market, or are inferior in terms of bargaining power, or are in possession of highly valued assets relative to males, we might expect to find a reluctance to employ them in jobs which involve supervision (particularly of men), promotion opportunities, relatively high wages and training. Further, one might predict that certain types of work will tend to be stereotyped as the preserve of one sex and that the sex of the appointee will correspondingly be a function of the previous job holder. To some extent this is reflected in the fact that in many of the female appointee cases, in particular, there were no applicants of the opposite sex, suggesting a self-selection on the part of the applicants themselves. To some extent this may reflect the fact that average earnings and wage scales in both labour markets were significantly lower where females were appointed. But there is also reason to believe that employer preferences are important. Thus some jobs were described as 'a man's job', and reference was made to the fact that a job involved contact with an all-male workforce 'on the shop floor'. Men were regarded as capable of dealing with difficult customers, more likely to have the general technical background needed for certain jobs, or more willing to do heavy work (such as packing orders in the warehouse), or to undertake shift-work (e.g. on switchboards or in computer work). A total of 86 appointments were made with respect to the 78 advertisements in the East Midlands, 54 (63%) being female and 32 (37%) male. Of the 70 appointments arising from advertisements which did not specify the gender required 25 (36%) were male appointees and 45 (64%) female. In interview recruitment managers expressed a preference for men with respect to 21 (26.9%) vacancies (23 appointments), a preference for women in 35 (44.9%) vacancies (39 appointments) and had no gender preference with respect to 22 (28.2%) vacancies (24 appointment). Of the 74 appointments in the West of Scotland 46 (62%) were female and 28 (38%) male. In 51 cases (69%) the gender required was not specified in the job advertisement. Of the 33 appointments (45%) arising where recruitment managers did not have a gender preference, 17 (52%) were male and 16 (48%) female. These latter figures might be influenced by the fact that some recruitment managers were interviewed after the introduction of the Sex Discrimination Act, but despite this, relatively more advertisements specified a gender preference in the West of Scotland.

Only five vacancies where women were acceptable in the East Midlands and ten in the West of Scotland involved the supervision of other workers and this in itself could explain the majority of female appointees. In only one case was a women appointed to a post requiring supervision of a mixed group of workers, but almost as high a percentage of men as of women supervised female employees. Thus, the supervision of women by men may not be seen as such a problem as the supervision of men by women. There does not appear to be a strong gender preference in jobs requiring the supervision of women and the preference for females is most marked in non-supervisory posts. Several of the respondents stated that supervision of males by females would be a problem – 'always a potential friction' or 'past experience shows a younger man may resent working for a woman' – and it was even suggested that women themselves do not seem to like supervising men and that men were more suited than women to supervising women (i.e. a clear case of role stereotyping).

Promotion from the post advertised was possible in 84 per cent of male and 52 per cent of female appointments in the East Midlands and 89.3 per cent of male vacancies and 71.7 per cent of female vacancies in the West of Scotland. Gender preferences were expressed more frequently when promotion prospects were not mentioned or not available, but this generally represented a preference for women in such posts. A significant number of respondents suggested that women were less ambitious than men and, therefore, were prepared to accept a job with little or no promotion prospects, whereas men were not. Thus many employers assume that women only want '9 to 5' jobs to fit in with present or future family commitments. In one case it was commented that 'the job does not have many promotion prospects. Any male who took the job would want day-release and would leave otherwise. Females, on the other hand, given regular real wage increases, would be content in such a job and have more limited ambitions.' One personnel manager observed that 'women are not so interested in self-fulfilment as men – they have other fulfilments. However, this is changing, partly due to women's attitudes, partly due to the legislation.'

Training opportunities were offered in 52.6 per cent of vacancies in the East Midlands and 40.6 per cent in the West of Scotland, 28.4 per cent, and 43.6 per cent respectively involving internal training arrangements and 9.0 per cent and 12.2 per cent respectively external training. Unlike in the East Midlands, there are, however, some paradoxical results in the West of Scotland. Whilst the fact that there is a preference for women chiefly where no training is provided can be easily explained, the similar result for male preferences cannot. Further, the gender preference in the no-training group appears to be even more marked for men than for women and the preference for women clearly greater than for men in the external training case (17.2% as opposed to nil). On the other hand, as in the East Midlands, a rather higher percentage of women than men were appointed where no training was offered and a much higher percentage of men (39.3% as opposed to 21.7%) where internal training was offered. Perhaps the higher percentage of female appointees in the external training case (15.2% as opposed to 7.1% of men) partly reflects the fact that in this case the costs of training are borne by the individual.

Sex stereotyping, as outlined above, would lead to the expectation that sex of previous job holder would predict sex of appointee. This can only be tested for a reduced sample since 18 per cent of the vacancies in the East Midlands and 27 per cent of the vacancies in the West of Scotland involved a new post. In both labour markets there is a tendency for a worker of one sex to be replaced by an applicant of the same sex, and not surprisingly there is a relationship between gender preference and sex of previous job-holder – 67 per cent of the male preferences in East Midlands and 55 per cent in the West of Scotland occurring where the previous incumbent was male and only 14 and 9 per cent respectively where female and 94 per cent of female preferences in the East Midlands and 79 per cent in the West of Scotland occurring when the previous incumbent was female as opposed to nil and 3 per cent respectively where male. Related to this question is the probability that, where a grade of work is regarded as the preserve of one sex, an appointment will be made of that sex. However – without allowance being made for unique jobs – whilst 40 per cent of females in the East Midlands and 46 per cent in the West of Scotland were appointed to predominantly female grades and only 6 per cent and 4 per cent respectively to predominantly male grades, the sex stereotyping appears to be much less marked on the male side with 10 per cent and 25 per cent of male appointments being made to female grades as opposed to only 14 per cent and 21 per cent to male grades.[8] This phenomenon may be explained by the fact, reported by a number of respondents, that declining employment opportunities for men were leading the latter to apply for what were considered to be previously female-type jobs. This asymmetry in relation to the sexes may also be a consequence of women – unlike men – leaving the labour market as employment opportunities decline.

In considering explanations for employers' gender preferences among applicants it is necessary to distinguish demand-side and supply-side factors. The former include the fact that women are more dexterous or perhaps less ambitious (i.e. superior or inferior in terms of performance potential) than men, or are cheaper. The latter emphasise the fact that only women (or men) present themselves for certain jobs. There is some suggestion that supply-side factors weigh more heavily than those on the demand side. In the latter case employers emphasised, in addition to the above features, the fact that men were preferred where there was an element of supervision, or where working conditions were unpleasant, involved dirty or dangerous conditions or contact with 'uncouth' male manual workers. Preference for men may also be based upon their lower propensity to quit relative to females, but in fact few of the respondents could provide statistics of the turnover in the job in question, though there was a detailed knowledge of the experience relating to previous job holders. This lack of formality with respect to turnover might indicate that this variable does not rate very highly in the hiring decision relative to other factors as far as these occupational groups are concerned. A major reason put forward for preferring females was the fact that they were more prepared than men to accept and apply themselves to boring, repetitive work. There was also some suggestion that women were more accurate and adaptable. In addition there seemed to be a strong preference for appointing women (or men) to jobs in which all existing employees were women (or men). But perhaps the main inducement for employers to continue employing women in certain jobs is the fact that they are cheaper than men on account of their lower transfer earnings. Indeed the wage offered serves as a signal to the applicant of the gender required since men (particularly those who are married) will not apply at that level of earnings. This is one reason why certain jobs became identified as 'men's' or 'women's' work. Any male applicant for a job classified in the latter group would be regarded as deficient in some way or other. Women would also fail to offer themselves for the former group of jobs because they lack the requisite experience, particularly in engineering where a knowledge of the various trades is sometimes important even in clerical jobs. There are thus powerful forces at work to perpetuate such self-selection.[9]

4. Selection bias: a case study of the entry of male and female students to an honours degree programme[10]

The selection of candidates, whether in hiring or promotion, is one of the ways in which discrimination can be practised either deliberately or unknowingly along the lines discussed in Chapter 2. It is important to examine, therefore, the methods that might be used to ascertain whether such selection bias exists. To illustrate a procedure which might be adopted we provide a case study concerning the admission of candidates to a degree course in economics at a British university. The principles involved are identical to those in any other selection process – such as the appointment of a person to a particular job – and the high quality of the data gives us the basis for an ideal illustration.

Before examining the particular case it is worthwhile considering the general framework within which this particular selection exercise takes place: Most applicants, whether domestic or foreign, seeking admission to a full-time first degree or diploma course at a U.K. university must apply through the Universities Central Council on Admissions (U.C.C.A.) which provides a standard form for the purpose. Statistics on the number of applications received by U.C.C.A. since 1975 are shown in Table 6.4. As can be seen, a much larger number of men than women apply in any one year although the proportion of female applicants has risen steadily over the period and stood at 38.5 per cent in 1980, compared with 33.9 per cent in 1975. It is interesting to speculate whether equal-pay and equal-opportunities legislation has contributed to the increase in the number of women seeking a university education. It will also be noted from Table 6.4 that a slightly higher proportion of women than men were accepted for university places in each year, with over half the female applications being successful. Such raw figures are, however, totally misleading as a guide to the existence of discrimination as they take no account of the qualities of the individual applicants. We take up this issue below.

It is also interesting to examine the distribution of applications by subject area where there are some clear, and perhaps not unexpected, differences between the sexes. The position for applications for admission in October 1980 is shown in Table 6.5. Thus, for example, whilst 25 per cent of male applications are for engineering and technology the corresponding figure for females is under 3 per cent. But, in this connection, it should be noted that there has been an increase in the proportion of female applicants seeking an engineering training in recent years, since for most of the 1970s the figure was around the one per cent level. In contrast nearly 22 per cent of female applications in 1979–80 were for languages, literature and area studies whereas such studies accounted for only 6 per cent of male applications. Also, whilst some 10 per cent of female applications are for arts subjects other than languages the corresponding figure for males is 5 per cent. Clearly a myriad of forces are at work in explaining these differences – ranging from actual or feared discrimination at work or university, through sex-role stereotyping at home or in the school, to the straightforward expression of preferences. It is not the purpose of this section to seek to offer a considered judgement on these issues, which spread far outside the scope of conventional economic analysis. Indeed the complexities provide justification, at least in part, for the relatively

Table 6.4: *Application to U.K. universities 1975–80*

	1975		1976		1977		1978		1979		1980	
	M	F	M	F	M	F	M	F	M	F	M	F
Accepted	46,074	25,137	47,572	26,360	49,651	28,204	50,486	30,044	50,401	31,997	51,028	33,667
Not accepted	40,861	19,406	46,044	22,331	50,353	25,408	51,007	25,969	53,955	30,009	52,504	31,155
Total	86,935	44,543	93,616	48,691	100,004	53,612	101,493	56,013	104,356	62,006	103,532	64,822
Percentage accepted	53.0	56.4	50.8	54.1	49.6	52.6	49.7	53.6	48.3	51.6	49.3	51.9

Sources: U.C.C.A. Annual Reports
U.C.C.A. Statistical Supplements

Table 6.5: *Candidates by preferred subjects of study, October* 1980

	Numbers		Percentage of total	
	Males	Females	Males	Females
Education	1,336	2,293	1.3	3.5
Medicine, dentistry and health	11,028	8,187	10.7	12.6
Engineering and technology	26,120	1,672	25.2	2.6
Agriculture, forestry and veterinary science	2,451	1,400	2.4	2.2
Science	20,787	9,903	20.1	15.3
Social, administrative and business studies	27,241	19,089	26.3	29.4
Architecture and other professional and vocational subjects	2,972	1,631	2.9	2.5
Languages, literature and area studies	6,289	14,087	6.1	21.7
Arts other than languages	5,308	6,560	5.1	10.1
Total	103,532	64,822	100	100

Source: U.C.C.A. Annual Report 1979–80

narrow approach to discrimination frequently adopted by economists. Nevertheless, until we have a grasp of some relatively simple issues we have no hope of progressing towards a real understanding of the more wide-scale problem. In the context of the current discussion, the key issue is to take one particular decision and analyse whether, in the light of the available information, the decision-maker(s) appears to be operating in a discriminatory manner. The particular question being asked in this case study is – once women have decided to apply for a particular course of study at a U.K. university is there any evidence that their applications are given discriminatory treatment? The method we shall use to seek to answer this question is of widespread applicability and it is in the method rather than the details of the particular case, that the interest lies.

The data we shall analyse relate to the applications to a medium-sized economics department in a British university during the year 1978–9, for admission in October 1979. The department concerned, in common with many others, made offers conditional on the forthcoming 'A' level examination results of the applicants and these offers were made almost entirely on the basis of the information contained in the standard U.C.C.A. application form. Testing or interviewing of candidates took place only in exceptional circumstances. In the particular year studied, the same conditional offer was made to all candidates irrespective of sex. In these circumstances discrimination by the department could only take the form of females (or males) having a lower probability of receiving an offer for given characteristics. One of the problems in measuring discrimination, as was discussed in Chapter 5, is that the outcome, be it wages, promotion or hiring, is determined by the reactions of both parties. If we are to identify discrimination we have to be sure that the offers made by one party to the other (e.g. the employer to employees) are different according to whether the recipient is male or female. Thus we have to ascertain that the employer makes a different offer for given characteristics to a female as compared with a male. In the case of university entrance, discrimination in this sense would be defined as males and females having a different probability of receiving an offer for identical characteristics as revealed by the U.C.C.A. form. Thus, by analysing the probability of receiving an offer it is possible to determine whether there is any evidence of discrimination against (or in favour of) women in the decision made. As with most other analyses of discrimination, it takes the revealed characteristics of the applicants as given and is unable to analyse whether these characteristics themselves are influenced by discrimination. The question at issue, therefore, is whether there is any evidence of a difference in treatment according to sex in the one particular decision being analysed. This is, in fact, the way in which a firm or other organisation should proceed if it wishes to assess whether its practices are discriminatory. It is also important to realise that the method is seeking to ascertain the criteria adopted by the decision-maker in reaching his or her conclusions. We do not seek to pass judgement on the reasonableness of these criteria although the revelation as to which characteristics appear to be important is a vital step in evaluating the attitude of the decision-maker.

In the case being analysed, the decision-maker faces a simple choice – either to offer or not to offer a conditional place to each applicant. The decision-maker is presumed to seek to obtain the 'best' students from amongst those who have applied, and assessment is based solely on the information contained in the application form. It was argued above that the data in this particular case offered an ideal illustration, and one of the major reasons for this is that both the researcher and the decision-maker have access to the same information. Thus the possibility that the researcher has missed something of significance to the decision is greatly reduced. For example, if interviews had been used in selection the researcher may have missed factors such as appearance, general manner etc. which could have been crucial in some cases. Even where the information is confined to a common written form such as the u.c.c.a. application, not all the difficulties are removed: handwriting, spelling and general presentation might be important, as might the list of interests that the candidates are invited to supply. There seemed no sensible way of making such factors operational and thus they were omitted from the analysis. One of the main problems of omitting important variables arises if they are correlated with those that are included in the relationship. In such a case the estimated effect of the included variables becomes unreliable. It does not seem likely that the omitted variables in this case will be highly correlated with those included. For example, the correlation, if any, between leisure pursuits and academic performance could go either way. It seems pretty safe to conclude that the problem of omitted variables is likely to be much less in this case than in many other studies of discrimination.

A few applications to the economics department were incomplete, or were from candidates with unusual qualifications. In such cases the data have been discarded. That left 364 applications, of which only 78 were from females. Statistics summarising the characteristics of these applicants together with a discussion of the measurement of the variables are given in Table 6.6. Some variables may reflect discrimination taking place elsewhere in society. Thus, for example, academic achievement or aspiration could be the result of discrimination within the schooling system or social pressures; school references could relay social prejudice. Whilst potentially important, these factors are clearly outside the control of the person concerned with making the offer decision.

Looking at Table 6.6 it will be observed that on average the female applicants have slightly better academic qualifications in that their

Table 6.6: *Applications to an economics department: summary statistics*

Continuous variables	Males		Females	
	Mean	Standard deviation	Mean	Standard deviation
Age	18.74	0.76	18.82	0.95
Number of 'O' levels	9.13	2.16	8.97	1.70
'O' level grades	2.57	0.65	2.28	0.56
Predicted 'A' level grades	3.00	0.91	2.75	0.83
Discrete variables	Percentage		Percentage	
Preference				
1st choice	39.5		44.9	
Reference				
Very good	18.9		24.4	
Good	47.9		57.8	
Other	33.2		21.8	
'A' level economics				
	80.4		73.1	
Offer made				
	61.5		71.8	
Number of applications	286		78	

Comments

Preference: The ranking of the department amongst the applicant's five stated choices. This is entered as a dummy with a value of 1 for first or joint first. A multiple dummy specification revealed all other values to be insignificant
Reference: Although classified into three groups, the empirical results showed no significant difference between the coefficients for good and very good and a single dummy was, therefore, entered to cover both categories
'O' level grades: Individual grades are entered as per their recorded value. Letter grades have been converted on the basis of A = 1.5; B = 2.5, etc.
'A' level grades: Letter grades are assigned the values A = 1; B = 2, etc.

'O' and 'A' level grades are somewhat better (reflected in a lower figure in the table). A greater proportion of women place the department as their first choice and have a good or very good reference. It will also be observed that over 70 per cent of female applicants received an offer whereas the corresponding figure for males was just over 60 per cent.

For those unfamiliar with the university system it is worth explaining why these proportions are so high – the department was looking for only 50–60 new students, yet over 230 offers were made. There are two main reasons for the number of offers being greatly in excess of the desired number of students. First, many applicants will receive offers from other departments since the u.c.c.a. application allows them up to five choices. Thus a proportion of the successful applicants will elect to study elsewhere. Second, the offers made by the department are conditional on achieving certain grades in the 'A' level examination which most students will be taking in the June of their year of application. A fairly high proportion of applicants who receive and accept a conditional offer from the department will be unsuccessful in attaining the necessary grades in the 'A' level examinations. In fact, from these 230 offers, the department was able to meet its target for admissions. This discussion does highlight the importance of looking at the offers and not the final acceptances in determining whether discrimination is practised since the outcome is to a considerable degree dependent on factors outside the control of the decision-maker.

Given that there are only two possible outcomes to each application the most appropriate approach is to analyse the probability that an individual will receive an offer. This probability depends on the revealed characteristics of the applicant and the weight attached to these characteristics by the decision-maker. The appropriate statistical technique for handling this problem is outlined in Appendix 6.3. As discussed in Chapter 5 one would ideally like to allow the effect of all the variables to differ according to the sex of the applicant but unfortunately in this case the size of the female sample (78) is not large enough to conduct such an exercise. As a first stage, therefore, in trying to ascertain which factors were important in determining the probability of an offer, the data for both sexes were combined with the results shown in Table 6.7. The variables included cover most of those available on the u.c.c.a. form.

Variables which are statistically significant on conventional criteria are marked with an asterisk in the table. It will be readily apparent that only a small number of the included variables appear to have any significant effect on the probability that an applicant will be offered a place. Factors like the place of residence of the applicant, the occupation of the parent and the type and number of subjects taken at 'A' level (with the exception of economics) all appear to have little influence on the outcome. The variables of significance are as follows: placing the department first choice[11] has a marked positive effect; the better the average 'O' level grade (with 1 being the highest) the more likely the candidate is to be offered a place

Table 6.7: *Logit analysis of offer decisions: restricted model*

Variable	Estimate	Variable	Estimate
Constant	-2.22	Good reference	$+1.67^*$
			(3.9)
Age[a]	-0.555	Economics 'A' level	$+1.812^*$
	(1.7)		(2.3)
South East region	$+0.37$	Maths 'A' level	$+0.804$
	(0.8)		(0.9)
Midlands region	-0.30	Maths and	-1.602
	(0.7)	economics 'A' level	(1.7)
First preference	$+1.727^*$	'A' levels already	-0.89
	(4.1)	taken	(1.6)
Professional parent	$+0.566$	General studies 'A'	$+0.363$
	(1.3)	level	(0.9)
Executive parent	$+0.093$	Work experience	-0.418
	(0.2)		(0.9)
Career specified	$+0.105$	3 'A' level subjects	$+0.823$
	(0.3)		(1.2)
Number of 'O' levels[a]	$+0.099$	Log likelihood	-104.7
	(1.0)		
'O' level grades[a]	-0.805^*	ρ^{2b}	0.56
	(2.0)		
Predicted 'A' level grades	-2.463^*	Degrees of freedom	334
	(6.0)		
Very good reference	$+1.37$		
	(1.8)		

Asymptotic t values in parentheses
* Significant at the 5% level
[a]Measured in terms of deviations about the overall mean
  All other variables are 1, 0 dummies.
[b] See Appendix 6.3 for definition

(the coefficient is negative since the lower the average the better the grade); the U.C.C.A. form in the year considered invited the school to enter the predicted 'A' level grades of the candidate and these predictions were assigned the values A = 1, B = 2 etc. Hence again the lower the value of the expected grades the better the performance, and the coefficient is correspondingly strongly negative. There is a high correlation between the applicant being given a very good reference by the school and the predicted 'A' level score. This relationship probably explains why a very good reference has an insignificant effect on the probability of receiving an offer but it does seem that the probability of being offered a place can be increased if the student is given a good reference (the second classification) holding the predicted 'A' level grades constant. Lastly, having studied economics at 'A' level appears to increase the probability that the application will be successful – at least for this particular department.

Having established which factors seem to be important in determining whether an application is successful, it is now possible to examine whether there is any evidence of discrimination in the admissions policy of the department. To answer this question it is necessary to allow the coefficients on each variable to differ between the sexes. Because this could not be done for all variables for the reason mentioned above, the variables which proved insignificant in Table 6.7 were initially dropped from the model and a new equation estimated. Various alternative formulations were tried and the variables which resulted in the best-fitting equation are shown in Table 6.8. No other combination of possible variables contributed significantly to the explanatory power of the equation. Model 2 in Table 6.8 allows all the coefficients to differ between the sexes by using interaction terms. The sex variable takes the value 1 if the applicant is female and zero if the applicant is male. Multiplying each of the variables by the sex variable creates a new set of variables which measure differences between the coefficients for males and females. If these interaction terms are statistically significant then there is evidence of differences in treatment between the sexes. Again, significant coefficients are marked with an asterisk and inspection of the results for model 2 shows that most of these interactions are insignificant indicating that each variable is given the same weight for both males and females. The only two interactions which proved significant were those concerned with the study of economics at 'A' level and the sex variable itself which, as shown in Chapter 5, indicates

Table 6.8: *Logit analysis of offer decisions*

	Model 1	Model 2
Constant	−1.94	−1.79
Sex (female = 1)	+2.98*	+3.06*
	(2.9)	(2.2)
Predicted 'A' level grades[a]	−2.52*	−2.45*
	(6.5)	(5.7)
Age	−0.73*	−0.54
	(2.5)	(1.7)
Preference (first = 1)	+1.64*	+1.58*
	(4.2)	(3.7)
Reference (good = 1)	+1.73*	+1.60*
	(4.3)	(3.7)
Economics 'A' level	+1.34*	+1.29
	(2.8)	(2.7)
'O' level grades	−0.47	−0.55
	(1.4)	(1.5)
Economics × sex	−3.38*	−4.03*
	(2.9)	(2.7)
Predicted 'A' level grades × sex		−0.79
		(0.7)
'O' level grades × sex		+0.46
		(0.4)
Age × sex		−1.07
		(1.2)
Preference × sex		+0.75
		(0.6)
Reference × sex		+0.74
		(0.6)
Log likelihood	107.5	106.3
ρ^2	0.55	0.55
Degrees of freedom	355	350

Asymptotic t values are in parentheses
* Significant at the 1% level
[a] 'A' level grades are scaled from 1 for an A to 6 for a fail

a difference in the intercept for the male and female equations. The results can be interpreted as follows: a girl who is of average age and has average 'A' level predictions has a higher probability of receiving an offer than an equivalent male but if she has studied economics at 'A' level her chances of being offered a place are somewhat lower than for a male in the same position.

Before reaching any conclusions however it is necessary to consider whether our equations offer a good fit to the data. In the standard regression analysis the usual criterion of goodness of fit is to examine the R^2 (the multiple correlation coefficient) and in our case, as shown in Appendix 6.3, there is an analogous statistic which is shown as ρ^2 in the tables. The values of 0.55 in Table 6.8 indicate that we have a fairly good fit. Alternatively, to get a better feel for the data, it is possible to look at the degree of misclassification implied by the estimates. If it is assumed that anyone with a predicted probability of 0.5 or more would have received an offer, Model 1 in Table 6.8 misclassifies 40 out of 364 cases. Of this total, 6 out of 78 females would be placed in the wrong category and 34 out of 286 males. Using both these criteria it would seem that Model 1 fits the data pretty well.

Predicted 'A' level grade is clearly the most important determinant of the probability of receiving an offer and there appears to be no difference in the treatment afforded the two sexes. The coefficient of the variable for preference shows that placing the department first choice has a positive favourable effect which again appears to be the same for males and females. Having a good reference also increases the probability as discussed earlier. Age has a negative coefficient indicating that those of above average age have a lower probability of being offered a place. This variable is picking up to some extent the fact that older students may have already taken 'A' levels and their results are known.

On balance, it does not seem that there is much evidence of any systematic sex discrimination in the admissions policy of this particular department but it is worthwhile examining the implications of the apparent differences in treatment for some characteristics. Perhaps the most suitable indicator is the effect of gender on marginal candidates. Taking a probability of 0.5 as the cut-off point, 12 males out of 286 would have moved from a probability above this figure to one below if they had been treated equally with women whereas 10 males would have moved in the opposite direction. If the 78 female applicants had been treated the same as males, 2 would have moved above 0.5 and 2 below. The net effect is, therefore, virtually zero and even the gross effect amounts to a negligible proportion of the total numbers involved. Thus, such an analysis reinforces the view that there is no evidence of any systematic discrimination.

The question remains as to whether the criteria used are fair. The only possible doubtful one is age, but others could reflect discrimination taking place elsewhere, e.g. in the provision of school references and the generating of 'A' level predictions. In the light of the results it would be difficult to argue that the decision-maker is using criteria which have a blatant discriminatory effect or that different weights are being systematically attached according to the sex of the applicant.

As mentioned above, the approach suggested in this case is applicable to a large number of circumstances within individual firms and organisations. As discussed in the chapter, selection criteria are of fundamental significance in determining the relative labour-market status of women and it is to be hoped that further studies along the lines suggested will greatly improve our understanding of the processes involved.

The emphasis in this chapter is on entry to the organisation as opposed to progression within it, though the analysis is equally applicable to the promotion decision. The evidence contained in this chapter points to the importance of role stereotyping illustrated by both the public employment service and the clerical vacancy studies. This highlights the relevance of using an approach such as that in the university entrance study which analyses the probability of a man or a woman receiving the offer of a place (or post). If studies are limited to what happens within organisations, this ignores the fact that certain individuals or groups may already have been excluded from the decision-making process.

APPENDIX 6.1

Regression analysis of personal characteristics in the West of Scotland Job Centre vacancies

An alternative way of considering the information on personal characteristics is to use a multiple regression model with required characteristics as the independent variables and sex of appointee as dependent variable. This enables us to answer the questions: what characteristics determine the 'maleness' or 'femaleness' (as determined by sex of person appointed) of a job? Have these characteristics altered significantly pre- and post-Act?

Appendix 6.1

Table 6.9 *Regression analysis, dependent variable the sex of the appointee to a vacancy ($M = 1$, $F = 0$), full-timers only (West of Scotland sample)*

	Value of coefficient	t value
Constant	0.554	
AGSPEC	0.080	3.69
OT	0.168	4.62
SHIFT	0.050	1.11
TR	0.022	0.51
EXP	− 0.70	2.29
TYPG	− 0.392	7.18
APPR	0.227	4.84
ED	− 0.032	0.36
PHYS	0.231	2.28
SPTASK	0.135	3.46
APP	− 0.276	8.39
FAM	− 0.195	1.30
HEAL	0.124	3.54
DEPY	− 0.052	1.53
DEXY	− 0.388	2.17
SOC	0.029	0.66
DRLIC	0.298	7.22

$R^2 = 0.489$
$N = 613$

Coding of Variables: AGSPEC = 1 if an age requirement is made, 0 otherwise; OT = 1 if overtime specified, 0 otherwise; SHIFT = 1 for shiftwork or special hours specified; TR = 1 if training is offered; EXP = 1 if experience is required; TYPG = 1 if typing is required, APPR = 1 if apprenticeship is required; ED = 1 if some educational qualification beyond school leaving (but not including typing or apprenticeship) is required; PHYS = 1 if physique is specified; SPTASK = 1 if special tasks (e.g. heavy lifting) are required; APP = 1 if good appearance is specified; FAM = 1 if family ties are specified; HEAL = 1 if good health is specified; DEPY = 1 if dependability is specified; DEXY = 1 if dexterity is specified; SOC = 1 if sociability is specified; DRLIC = 1 if a driving licence is required

In the regression the dependent variable is a binary variable, taking the value of 1 (0) for vacancies in which a man (woman) was appointed. The use of such a dependent variable raises statistical problems because one of the assumptions of ordinary least-squares regression is violated, namely that the error term should have a constant variance, i.e. should be homoscedastic. In such a situation a more correct procedure than regression is logit analysis which involves transforming the dependent variable so that it becomes continuous. Unfortunately at the time this part of the study was conducted an appropriate program was not available and we report here the regression results, which for the reason above must be treated with caution.

Results are given in Table 6.9 for the whole sample, pooling observations pre- and post-Act. When regressions were run on pre-Act and post-Act observations separately, a test for the significance of differences in coefficients showed the differences to be insignificant. Consequently, pooling the observations is appropriate. Thus we cannot reject the hypothesis that the characteristics determining the maleness or femaleness of a vacancy have not changed since the implementation of the Sex Discrimination Act.

Looking at the coefficients, these are to be interpreted in terms of the probability of the appointee being male. Thus if typing was specified this reduces the probability that the appointee would be a male by 39 per cent. Broadly speaking the pattern of coefficients bears out the impression gained from inspection of Table 6.3. Particularly interesting is the strong influence of supply-side factors in determining which sex is appointed, as shown by the size and significance of the coefficients on the typing and apprenticeship variables. The *t* statistics and the sign of the coefficients show that age, overtime, apprenticeship, physique, special tasks, health and driving licence are male appointee characteristics and experience, typing, appearance and dexterity are female appointee characteristics.

APPENDIX 6.2

Regression analysis of determinants of hiring in clerical occupations

Despite the relatively small sample size it was felt that multiple regression analysis might throw additional light on the hiring process.

Appendix 6.2

The dependent variable is a binary variable taking the value of unity if a woman was appointed or preferred. (For the statistical deficiencies of this method see Appendix 6.1.) This variable is regressed on variables such as whether the job involved supervision, or was high paying, or was previously held by a male. This method is an alternative way of analysing relationships, such as whether the sex of the previous incumbent influences that of the current appointee. It has the advantage that some other factors can simultaneously be 'held constant', and the t values enable a judgement to be made as to the strength of the relationship.

In Table 6.10, five regressions are given, using various arguments to explain sex of appointee or preference for women. The pattern is broadly as the tabular analysis already covered would lead us to expect. However it might come as something of a surprise to see how significant the negative impact of the vacancy's wage rate is for the probability of a woman being appointed, *ceteris paribus*. This is seen in regressions 1, 3 and 5, but is more striking in regression 1, since more factors are held constant. From regression 1 we see that a rise of £500 (one standard deviation) in the wage attached to the vacancy reduces the probability of a woman being employed by 20 percentage points, *ceteris paribus*.

The other variable which appears to be important is the sex of the previous holder. This is apparent from regressions 2, 3, 4 and 5. The fact of the previous incumbent being female appears powerfully to dictate that the new incumbent will be female. This is so, moreover, even holding the wage constant, as regressions 3 and 5 indicate. These results confirm that patterns of employment are well entrenched, and likely to be difficult to change. It must be emphasised, however, that these results have no bearing on whether these patterns are in some sense 'justified' or not.

APPENDIX 6.3

Estimation of the probability of receiving an offer

In estimating the factors which determine the probability that any individual applicant will receive an offer it has to be recognised that the dependent variable is dichotomous (offer $= 1$; no offer $= 0$). The relationship between the probability of the ith individual receiving an offer (P_i) and his/her vector of personal characteristics (x_i) may

119

Table 6.10: *Determinants of sex of appointee or sex preference*
(Dependent variable = 1 if a woman appointed, 0 otherwise)

Equation 1: West of Scotland – sex of appointee

Constant	*Supervisor*	*Promotion*	*Wage*	*Training*	*Qualif.*	*Exper.*	*Test*
1.5	-0.106	-0.037	-0.0004	-0.074	-0.057	0.237	-0.024
(9.1)	(1.0)	(0.32)	(4.91)	(0.79)	(0.52)	(1.60)	(1.64)
	0.34	0.78	£2109	0.41	0.55	0.81	0.11

Equation 2: West of Scotland – sex of appointee

Constant	*No prev. holder*	*Prev. holder male*
0.888	-0.46	-0.48
(12.0)	(3.74)	(4.00)

Equation 3: West of Scotland – sex of appointee

Constant	*Female grade*	*Prev. holder female*
1.23	0.035	0.307
(6.99)	(0.38)	(3.38)

Equation 4: East Midlands – sex of appointee

Constant	*Male grade*	*Prev. holder female*	*Wage*
0.35	-0.52	0.51	-0.00036
	(3.12)	(5.59)	(5.23)

Equation 5: East Midlands – preference for females

Constant	*Female grade*	*Prev. holder female*	*Wage*
0.43	0.29	0.46	-0.0002
	(2.52)	(4.64)	(2.19)

t statistics are in parentheses

be written as

$$P_i = F(x_i'\beta) \qquad i = 1,\ldots, n \tag{6.1}$$

where β is a vector of unknown coefficients.

It is necessary to specify the functional form of F, where $F(t)$ denotes a cumulative distribution function. If $F(t)$ is taken to be the cumulative density function of the logistic distribution the following equations result:

$$F(t) = (1 + e^{-t})^{-1} \qquad -\infty < t < \infty \tag{6.2}$$

combining (6.1) and (6.2)

$$P_i = \frac{1}{1 + e^{-x_i'\beta}} \tag{6.3}$$

or

$$\ln\left(\frac{P_i}{1 - P_i}\right) = x_i'\beta \tag{6.4}$$

Where there is non-repetition of trials, as in the case here, equation (6.4) is termed the conditional logit model.[12] An alternative, commonly used form for $F(t)$ is the cumulative density function of the normal distribution, in which case it is termed probit analysis. The logistic distribution is a good approximation to the normal and estimates of β obtained by using the two distributions are generally close except for a multiplicative factor.

Experiments were made with the data here, using both functional forms, and the general result was confirmed. Since there may be good reasons for preferring the logistic function[13] only results obtained from using this distribution are reported in the text.

McFadden[14] has shown that in the logit model a coefficient of determination can be defined that is analogous to the multiple correlation coefficient, R^2, in ordinary least-squares regression. Thus,

$$\rho^2 = 1 - \frac{L(\hat{\beta})}{L(\hat{\beta}^H)} \tag{6.5}$$

where $\hat{\beta}^H$ is the maximum likelihood estimator under the null hypothesis and $\hat{\beta}$ is the unconstrained maximum likelihood estimator. If $\hat{\beta}$ is zero then ρ^2 lies between 0 and 1 in the same way as R^2. The value of ρ^2 has been included in the tables in the text.

7
Conclusions

In this book we have shown that a myriad of complex forces lead to the differences in earnings and occupations which exist between men and women. Only some of these relate to any discrimination at the workplace, whether practised by employers or by employees. If all such discrimination were to be removed overnight the improvement in average female earnings would be substantial, but the average would still be likely to remain around 80 per cent of male earnings.

Looking at what happens on average may, however, be seriously misleading as there are substantial differences between individuals within both sexes. Some will have greater aptitude or skills, or have undertaken more training or may be more highly motivated. The acquisition of skills is not free and can involve the individual and his/her employer in considerable costs. The creation of skills in this way results in the formation of human capital and an understanding of this concept is a vital step towards comprehending the similarities and differences between male and female labour-force behaviour. It is an incontrovertible fact that the majority of women get married and many women, whether married or not, raise children. And in our own and most other societies the woman tends to do the bulk of the work associated with the care of children. If this pattern is to change it requires a fundamental review of attitudes well beyond the scope of any equal-opportunities legislation. Of course, the provision – and quality – of public-sector services, crèche and day-care facilities are of fundamental importance in giving women the chance to relinquish these activities in favour of work in the labour market. But it remains true that certainly in the early years of a child's life many parents still prefer to look after their own children, regardless of the fact that there may be adequate child-care facilities outside the home. Correspondingly, many women take time away from market work, often for several years, to look after children, and then return at a later date. As Hakim notes,[1] this two-phase work profile is of fairly recent origin in Britain and is most noticeable in the post-Second World War period. If attitudes to child care and the division of household activities between the sexes change substantially this will have a profound effect on the future relative labour-market experience of the two sexes.

During the period of absence from market work there will be a tendency for skills to depreciate through lack of use. Also, as technical change progresses, skills tend to become obsolete, with little opportunity to restore their value. As we saw in Chapter 2, recent American evidence casts some doubt on the magnitude of any depreciation which takes place; but the fact remains that without day-to-day practice and exposure to new techniques there is little chance for any skills to be enhanced. Further, over the next few years it is likely that we shall see sweeping changes in many of the work environments, such as offices which are currently dominated by women, as the microprocessor revolution gains momentum. Indeed, the fact that skills are now changing rapidly within the labour market may offer an opportunity for women who are engaged in household activities to equip themselves with the new skills by taking appropriate courses on a part-time basis and returning to the labour market with an advantage over those who have remained in full-time work.

However, absence from the labour force means not only that no income is being earned to recoup the costs of any training, but also the value of skill acquired in the past is itself diminishing to some extent. These facts make it quite rational for women to be less willing to invest in the acquisition of skills. Thus we find that more men than women tend to pursue education to a higher level; and that women have less incentive to begin careers which involve low initial salaries for the benefit of higher incomes in the future. Anyone familiar with the simple rules of investment appraisal will recognise that it is the returns in the early years that are most crucial in determining the success of the venture; and it is in these early years that women are most likely to leave market work and drastically reduce the return on their investment. For similar reasons, employers might also be less willing to finance the training of women although it has to be recognised that whilst the male may remain in the labour force he may be likely to leave any particular employment. Thus it may be that a particular woman is a better bet than most males.

Here the crucial issue is the selection of individual employees and we emphasize this point in Chapter 6. Also, as we noted in Chapter 2, there is the problem of obtaining reliable information, prior to employment, about the potential performance of any individual worker.

The problem of information explains at least in part why there might be a tendency for employers to make decisions on the basis of the expected characteristics of a readily identified group of workers – and gender is an easy way of splitting people into groups. Thus, if employers believe that women as a group are less reliable, more prone to absence and more likely to leave, they may prefer to employ males. As we pointed out in Chapter 2 this cannot necessarily be regarded as discrimination in terms of the definition we have adopted and, given the costs of obtaining information, an alternative strategy may be rather expensive. If employers' beliefs are incorrect, where competitive forces operate, one would expect their attitudes to change over time. It is commonly argued that periods of buoyant demand are the most favourable for this process to take place and, unfortunately for women, the period since the passing of the Sex Discrimination Act has been marked by anything but buoyant demand.

We have emphasised that the family, and its associated responsibilities, has an important effect on the position of women in employment. Such a factor has to be taken as given in any analysis of discrimination at the workplace. It also suggests that there are likely to be differences between individuals according to their marital status, and in Chapter 5 we suggested how this fact might be used to gain a clearer picture of the extent of discrimination. There we stated that the most appropriate comparison is likely to be between single men and single women, and we reported on studies that showed that sex discrimination in earnings amounted to around 10 per cent. This figure, although substantial, is considerably less than many people seem to imagine.

These studies mainly used data from periods before the Sex Discrimination Act; it will interesting to see the results produced by studies in the mid-1980s. But it should be remembered that any effects of the legislation are likely to take some time to filter through the system. This is one of the reasons why, in Chapter 6, we stress the importance of hiring and promotion decisions and present a methodology, in some detail, for assessing the discriminatory component in such decisions. Earnings data tend to pick up the effects of discrimination that might have taken place in the past, whereas current hiring and promotion decisions reflect the present state of attitudes and behaviour. Thus, for example, it is often quoted that in the Civil Service there are no female permanent secretaries and only 3 per cent of deputy secretaries are women. This reflects decisions taken over a period of more than 30 years. If discrimination was practised in the recruitment and promotion procedures in the early 1950s then there will be few women available for upward promotion in the 1980s. Any change in attitudes will take 25 to 30 years before it is reflected in the crude data. It is important for decision-makers to ensure that they are not currently reflecting any unwarranted sex bias in their decisions and we come back to this, below.

The fact that there are many issues involved, and that discrimination at work is not necessarily the major factor, should not lead us into complacency. It is important that all economic resources are used effectively and sex discrimination impairs the efficiency of the economy, as well as introducing inequities. The bulk of the book has been concerned with the problems of defining and measuring discrimination at the workplace. We have pointed out that there are many possible definitions but that regard should be paid to differences in performance. Correspondingly we have argued that it is important to control for differences in individual characteristics to gain some idea of the magnitude of any discrimination. Most of our research which we report in this book has been concerned with this issue, so it is appropriate to consider the main lessons that can be learned from such studies.

1. The major lessons to be learned

In Chapter 4 we provided a review of the developments in the law relating to discrimination in Britain. We reported the conclusions of the main tribunal and court decisions, and their implications. The scope of the legislation is being widened under the influence of European law. One major implication is, therefore, that management will need to develop more positive measures to monitor and tackle the discriminatory practices which take place within their organisations. At the same time the trade unions will need to keep abreast of developments and keep their own policies and attitudes under review. As we showed in Chapter 2, despite the Equal Pay Act having been in existence for over ten years, and the Sex Discrimination Act for over five years, there is still considerable ignorance of the law. It seems that cases in clear breach of the legislation are not recognised by the women concerned and the relevant unions. There are signs that pressure for women's rights might increase. The decline in their rate of progress in terms of average earnings at the end of the 1970s has not gone unnoticed by the principal parties; although, as we pointed out in Chapter 3, it is not clear how much of the relative improvement in the mid-1970s was due to equal-pay and equal-opportunities legislation and how much to other factors such as flat-rate incomes policies. As expectations about progress fail to be realised, one might expect increased pressure for action. We have taken care to point out throughout the book, however, that high expectations of the success of legislation might have been based on false hopes. We have argued that for many reasons substantial gains were not to be expected, and evidence from other countries, particularly the United States, would support this claim.

It also needs to be recognised that market forces do operate. The Equal Opportunities Commission has noted in its annual report for 1980[2] that the past five years have been the most unhelpful and least propitious five years in the post-war period in which to embark upon the task of promoting equal opportunities for women. It is also apparent that women are bearing a greater brunt of the recession than men. Their relative unemployment has risen and there seems to have been a substantial fall in part-time jobs. But a study of elementary economics would suggest that these features are not surprising. Just as minimum wage laws tend to increase unemployment amongst the disadvantaged groups they are designed to protect, so equal-pay and equal-opportunities legislation tends to price some women out of the labour market. As noted in Chapter 2, this, and other legislation, has tended to make women relatively more expensive and it is not too surprising, therefore, that they are hit harder by recession, although until recently employment in the female-dominated service sector has not declined as much as in manufacturing industry.

All these facts are painful and they come at a time when the efficacy of anti-discrimination legislation is being questioned. The probability of a tribunal hearing for any one employer has been fairly remote as we showed in Chapter 4 and the number of cases under the Equal Pay Act is declining rapidly. The Equal Opportunities Commission has argued that no further progress is possible under the existing legislation unless its provisions are considerably toughened. Michael Foot referred in a speech in 1981 to the possible introduction of a Minister for Equality in a future Labour government. As we discussed in Chapter 4, the Equal Opportunities Commission has proposed a code of conduct on equality of opportunity and we have already outlined the main features of this proposal.

For many reasons, therefore, we see the issue of equality of opportunity remaining in the public interest. So how would studies such as have been reported in this book help those concerned? The main contribution which can be made is to provide a sophisticated guide to monitoring, measuring and remedying any discriminatory practices. We have stressed – because it does not often seem to be recognised in public pronouncements – that the simple collection and analysis of broad statistics is not sufficient to answer the question whether discrimination exists. It is a useful start, but much more is required. In Chapters 5 and 6 we have outlined the broad principles which can be adopted and warned of the main pitfalls. In the presentation of cases before United States courts evidence of the type we have suggested is frequently used. As we note in the following section, there is pressure to change the burden of proof in the existing legislation and exercises of the kind we have suggested would be a useful stage in proving or defending any allegation. Of course, as we have recognised, any one case concerns a specific individual, and further evidence would be essential to prove or disprove any allegation of specific discrimination. The emphasis on the general rather than the specific is one of the main differences between the legal and economic approaches to the issue of sex discrimination. Nevertheless interchange between the two professions is widening, the number of law and economics journals is increasing and there is considerable evidence of fruitful co-operation.[3]

We wish to emphasise the importance of the collection and analysis of relevant statistics and the necessity of making a distinction in these studies not only on the basis of gender but also on the basis of marital status and/or the presence of children. Not only is this important because the Sex Discrimination Act specifically prohibits discrimination on the basis of marriage, but also it is through this distinction that one may be better able to identify any discriminatory component. The estimation of earnings functions of the type we discussed in Chapter 5 or studies of hiring and promotion which we considered in Chapter 6 also need information on the individual characteristics of the actual or potential employees, covering factors such as education, training and experience. What is required is information on variables that can be used to correct for differences that are not a consequence of discrimination. It is important, however, that these characteristics are related to the requirements of the job. This issue is particularly relevant to the question of indirect discrimination and it is necessary to consider the reasonableness of the characteristics which are used by the organisation in reaching its decisions. Identification of these characteristics through the type of study suggested is itself an exercise which could be of considerable relevance to decision-makers.

It is clear from the legal decisions reported in Chapter 4 that it is inadequate for employers to rest their case on broad generalisations concerning any particular group of workers. In the case of alleged discrimination, evidence on the level of productivity of individual workers is required to disprove the allegation that differences in pay and occupational level are based on sex. An equal-opportunities policy, therefore, implies the collation of detailed statistics. The relevant measurement problems have been discussed in detail throughout the book.

We can summarise the implications for management and trade unions of the developments suggested in this book in three points: (i) the parties need to ensure that they are familiar with the precise terms of the legislation so that they do not practise discrimination through ignorance; (ii) detailed information is required on a regular basis on the distribution of men and women in each organisation; (iii) it would be prudent to develop an explicit equal-opportunities policy which is communicated to all levels of the organisation and which is monitored on a regular basis using to advantage the techniques we have outlined.

The overall lesson is perhaps best summed up by a quotation from the paper by Siebert and Sloane[4] who have used the approach suggested:

> As for the policy, the methodology of this paper could
> provide the basis for a defence against a charge of
> discrimination. Here it should be noted that even
> inconclusive results are helpful in suggesting that
> discrimination is not of major significance. Certainly the

case studies bring out the danger of attempting to draw conclusions about the relative treatment of men and women merely by reference to mean levels of earnings and proportionate distributions among occupations. The difficulties frequently experienced by the courts in determining whether discrimination has taken place might well be reduced by the adoption of the techniques utilised in this paper.

2. The role of legislation

If on careful analysis it is apparent that discrimination at the workplace is not the principal explanation of the earnings and occupational distribution of women, it is not surprising that the legislation on equal pay and equal opportunities does not seem to have had a marked impact in either Britain or the United States. The British legislation, much criticised when it was introduced, does not allow reverse discrimination, except in a narrow sense relating to training (which does not seem to have been much used in practice), to correct any past unfavourable treatment. There is, for example, no provision for quotas or guidelines on the lines of an affirmative action programme. It seems unlikely that any such provisions would be introduced in Britain in the foreseeable future and the evidence from the United States, reviewed in Chapter 2, is not particularly encouraging. But, as we have discussed earlier in this chapter, there will undoubtedly be increased pressure for some toughening of the British legislation, and to conclude the book it would be appropriate to consider briefly the main criticisms and proposed remedies.

In their review of the operation of both Acts, Snell, Glucklich and Povall[5] reach the following conclusions as to the ineffectiveness of legislation:

> our findings highlight the lack of commitment to and action on equal pay and opportunities by both management and unions at work-place level. Employers faced difficult economic circumstances and other problems at the time the legislation came in. In the absence of any real pressure for change from women and unions within the organisations and from the Equal Opportunities Commission outside them, many employers chose to do as little as possible and to keep changes, costs and disruption to a minimum. Unions, when they

played a positive role, were a critical positive factor, but they more often played an (equally important) negative or passive role in implementation. Women, before the end of 1975, were largely ignorant of their rights and in most cases were not in a position to influence the implementation of the legislation. Even where they became more aware after the legislation came into force in 1975 they still lacked the necessary bargaining power and experience to bring about collective action within the work-place.

In our view, the authors of this study were expecting rather more from the legislation than it could deliver and do not seem to have taken into full consideration the many important economic forces at work. Nevertheless their conclusions do illustrate the prevailing attitudes and progress that they detected from their detailed case studies. So, if the law has been relatively ineffective, what viable proposals are there for its modification?

A probable major change in the foreseeable future is likely to relate to the provisions of the Equal Pay Act. It will be recalled that its main provision is for equal pay for the same or broadly similar work. Thus the requirement is to find a male doing such work and it has been argued for some time that such a requirement is unnecessarily onerous. As we noted in Chapter 4. Article 119 of the Treaty of Rome lays down equal pay for equal work and in February 1975 a directive of the Council of Ministers defined equal work as meaning identical work or work of equal value. The European Commission has taken the view that the application of the principle of equal pay has still not been fully implemented and in March 1978 announced its intention to introduce infringement procedures against a number of member states including the U.K. If the Court upholds the Commission's view it is likely that the British legislation will need to be modified and, if the concept of equal pay for work of equal value is introduced, the area of comparison will be widened considerably. Of course, it would be up to the tribunals and courts to interpret the law, and the precise implications of the change are not clear. The introduction of such a clause which emphasises the value of the work would make it even more essential for organisations to conduct analyses along the lines we have suggested.

The indirect discrimination provisions of the Sex Discrimination Act are a significant, if perhaps little understood, part of the legislation. The recent finding of the European Court of Justice, that indirect discrimination provisions apply to the Equal Pay Act, would deal with cases where jobs depend on factors – such as length of service – which militate against women who leave work to have a family. The problem here is one of interpretation since presumably, as under the Sex Discrimination Act, the employer could still claim justification for the practice. We have argued that on economic grounds length of service is likely to be a highly relevant variable which could justify different treatment. Again the concept of human capital is central to the argument. Thus we would advise the parties that the use of arguments based soundly on economic analysis with its associated statistical investigation could be of vital significance in proving or disproving any claim of discrimination.

The Equal Opportunities Commission has also made a number of other recommendations to the Home Secretary (as outlined in Chapter 4), many of which are concerned with issues wider than discrimination at the place of work. But, even if the law is 'toughened' in the ways outlined, will it make much difference? Our view is that one really must examine the more fundamental factors at work and be aware of the economic implications of these forces. It is clear to us that, in explaining the labour-market position of women, discrimination at the workplace is less significant than factors that are deep-rooted in social attitudes and behaviour and which may themselves have economic causes. We have to repeat that what happens within and to the family is to a large degree the crucial issue. Family responsibilities have widespread ramifications throughout the labour market. Indeed, if there were to be complete role-reversal, such that it was males who left work to look after children and females who had full labour-force participation over their working life, we would predict that in the long run male average earnings would be substantially lower than female average earnings and that men would be concentrated in lower-paid and lower-status jobs. This would not arise from any discrimination practised by women but simply from the value of the services supplied to the labour market. Market earnings result from the interaction of two sets of forces – those reflecting the demand side and those emanating from the supply side. Discrimination is a demand-side phenomenon and the problem in evaluating and monitoring discrimination is to determine how much of the difference between the earnings (or occupation level, hiring rate or promotion rate) of two or more groups of workers is due to differences in their supply characteristics and how much to pure discrimination by employers or members of other groups. Our own and other studies would suggest that supply-side differences are the major contributory factors. Legislation can remove the more blatant abuses, but by itself it should not be expected to produce a radical alteration in the relative position of women in the labour market. If women are to approach the earnings and occupational levels of men, it is necessary for a complete reappraisal of social attitudes to take place; and in particular there has to be a reallocation of time between housework in its broadest sense, market work and leisure between the sexes. The question still remains whether such a re-allocation would benefit the family. If it does, and as technology makes it increasingly possible, we might see a substantial improvement in the relative earnings of women over the next few decades. But it will be a slow process. On the other hand, if there really are economic advantages in the family unit as presently organised, it is likely that women in general will continue to earn substantially less than men and remain in lower-grade occupations despite the efforts of equal-opportunities legislation.

Notes

Chapter 1 Introduction

1 For a summary see, for example, B. Chiplin and P. J. Sloane, *Sex Discrimination in the Labour Market*, Macmillan, London, 1976.
2 R. C. Battalio, J. H. Kagel and M. O. Reynolds, 'A Note on the Distribution of Earnings and Output per Hour in an Experimental Economy', *Economic Journal*, Vol. 88, No. 352, December 1978.

Chapter 2 Economic and legal perspectives on discrimination

1 K. E. Boulding, 'Toward a Theory of Discrimination', in Phyllis A. Wallace (ed.), *Equal Employment Opportunity and the A. T and T. Case*, M.I.T. Press, Cambridge, Mass. 1976.
2 See T. Sowell, *Race and Economics*, David McKay Co., New York, 1975.
3 Cynthia B. Lloyd and Beth T. Niemi, *The Economics of Sex Differentials*, Columbia University Press, New York, 1979.
4 G. Becker, *The Economics of Discrimination*, University of Chicago Press, Chicago, 1957.
5 See e.g. L. C. Thurow, *Generating Inequality*, Macmillan, London, 1976; and B. Chiplin and P. J. Sloane, *Sex Discrimination in the Labour Market*, Macmillan, London, 1976.
6 See D. J. Aigner and G. G. Cain, 'Statistical Theories of Discrimination in Labour Markets', *Industrial and Labour Relations Review*, Vol. 30, No. 2, January 1977; and W. S. Siebert and P. J. Sloane, 'The Measurement of Sex and Marital Status Discrimination at the Workplace', *Economica*, Vol. 48, 1981.
7 For example because of monopsony in the labour market.
8 B. Chiplin and P. J. Sloane, 'Sexual Discrimination in the Labour Market', *British Journal of Industrial Relations*, Vol. XII, No. 3, November 1974, reprinted in Alice H. Amsden (ed.), *The Economics of Women and Work*, Penguin Books, Harmondsworth, 1980.
9 J. Stiglitz, 'Approaches to the Economics of Discrimination', *American Economic Review, Papers and Proceedings*, Vol. 63, No. 2, May 1973.

10 C. K. Rowley, 'Social Sciences and Law: The Relevance of Economic Theories', *Oxford Journal of Legal Studies*, No. 3, 1981.

11 G. Becker, *The Economics of Discrimination*.

12 Chapter 2, P. A. Wallace and A. M. LaMond, *Women, Minorities and Employment Discrimination*, Lexington Books, Lexington, Mass., 1977.

13 See, for example, W. G. Shepherd and S. G. Levin, 'Managerial Discrimination in Large Firms', *Review of Economics and Statistics*, Vol. LV, No. 4, November 1973; and M. H. Medoff, 'Market Power and Employment Discrimination: A Comment', *Journal of Human Resources*, Vol. XV, No. 2, 1980.

14 R. Franklin and M. Tanzer, 'Traditional Micro-economic Analysis of Racial Discrimination: A Critical View and Alternative Approach', *Industrial and Labor Relations Review*, Vol. 21, No. 3, April 1968.

15 See for example P. Turnbull and G. Williams, 'Sex Differentials in Teachers' Pay', *Journal of the Royal Statistical Society*, Part II, Ser. A, Vol. 37, 1974; M. A. Ferber and B. Kordick, 'Sex Differentials in the Earnings of Ph.D.s', *Industrial and Labor Relations Review*, Vol. 32, January 1978; R. H. Frank, 'Why Women Earn Less: The Theory and Estimation of Differential Overqualification', *American Economic Review*, Vol. 68, No. 3, June 1978; and M. Corcoran and G. J. Duncan, 'Work History, Labour Force Attachment and Earnings Differences between Races and Sexes', *Journal of Human Resources*, Vol. XIV, No. 1, Winter 1979.

16 For the development of this theory see R. H. Frank, 'Why Women Earn Less'.

17 C. Greenhalgh, 'Male–Female Wage Differentials in Great Britain: Is Marriage an Equal Opportunity?', *Economic Journal*, Vol. 90, No. 360, December 1980.

18 C. Greenhalgh, 'Male–Female Wage Differentials in Great Britain'.

19 J. Mincer and S. Polachek, 'Family Investments in Human Capital: Earnings of Women', *Journal of Political Economy*, Vol. 82, March/April 1974 and J. Mincer and S. Polachek, 'Women's Earnings Re-examined', *Journal of Human Resources*, Vol. XII, No. 1, 1978.

20 S. Polachek, 'Occupational Segregation Among Women: Theory, Evidence and a Prognosis', in C. B. Lloyd, E. S. Andrews and C. L. Gilroy (eds.), *Women in the Labour Market*, Columbia University Press, New York, 1979.

21 See P. Turnbull and G. Williams, 'Sex Differentials in Teachers' Pay'. For the U.S. evidence see M. Corcoran and G. J. Duncan, 'Work History, Labour Force Attachment and Earnings Differences between Races and Sexes'; and E. B. Jones and J. E. Long, 'Human Capital and Labour Market Employment. Additional Evidence for Women', *Journal of Human Resources*, Vol. XIV, No. 2, Spring 1979.

22 M. Corcoran, 'Work Experience, Labour Force Withdrawals, and

Women's Wages: Empirical Results Using the 1976 Panel of Income Dynamics', in C. B. Lloyd, E. S. Andrews and C. Gilroy (eds.), *Women in the Labour Market.*

23 G. J. Duncan and S. Hoffman, 'On-the-Job Training and Earnings Differences by Race and Sex', *Review of Economics and Statistics*, Vol. LXI, No. 4, November 1979.

24 See, for example, W. S. Comanor, 'Racial Discrimination in American Industry', *Economica*, Vol. 40, November 1973; M. H. Medoff, 'On Estimating the Relationship between Discrimination and Market Structure: A Comment', *Southern Economic Journal*, Vol. 46, No. 4, April 1980; S. M. Oster, 'Industry Differences in the Level of Discrimination Against Women', *Quarterly Journal of Economics*, Vol. LXXIX, No. 2, May 1975; W. R. Johnson, 'Racial Wage Discrimination and Industrial Structure', *The Bell Journal of Economics*, Vol. 9, No. 1, Spring 1978; and E. T. Fujii and J. M. Trapani, 'On Estimating the Relationship between Discrimination and Market Structure', *Southern Economic Journal*, January 1978.

25 For a discussion see any text on industrial organisation such as D. A. Hay and D. J. Morris, *Industrial Economics: Theory and Evidence*, Oxford University Press, 1979.

26 See, for example, A. D. Krueger, 'The Economics of Discrimination', *Journal of Political Economy*, Vol. 71, October 1973; and L. C. Thurow, *Poverty and Discrimination*, Brookings Institution, Washington D.C., 1969.

27 K. E. Boulding, 'Toward a Theory of Discrimination'.

28 F. Y. Edgeworth, 'Equal Pay to Men and Women for Equal Work', *Economic Journal*, Vol. 31, 1922; B. R. Bergmann, 'The Effect on White Incomes of Discrimination in Employment', *Journal of Political Economy*, Vol. 79, 1971; and B. R. Bergmann, 'Occupational Segregation, Wages and Profits when Employers Discriminate by Race or Sex', *Eastern Economic Journal*, Vol. 1, No. 2–3, April–July 1974.

29 J. E. Roemer, 'Divide and Conquer: Microfoundations of a Marxian Theory of Wage Discrimination', *The Bell Journal of Economics*, Vol. 10, No. 2, Autumn 1979.

30 Formerly the Industrial Arbitration Board.

31 M. W. Snell, P. Glucklich and M. Povall, *Equal Pay and Opportunities: A Study of the Implementation and Effects of the Equal Pay and Sex Discrimination Acts in 26 Organisations*, Research Paper No. 20, Department of Employment, April 1981.

32 I. Papps, 'Equal Pay and Female Unemployment', *The Journal of Economic Affairs*, Vol. 1, No. 1, October 1980.

33 O. Ashenfelter, 'Comment', *Industrial and Labor Relations Review*, July 1976.

34 See A. H. Beller, 'The Impact of Equal Opportunity Laws on the Male–Female Earnings Differential'; E. Lazear, 'Male–Female Wage Differentials: Has the Government Had Any Effect?'; and comments by I. V. Sawhill, P. A. Wallace and M. R. Killingsworth in C. B. Lloyd, E. S. Andrews and C. L. Gilroy (eds.), *Women in the Labour Market.*
35 See note 34.

Chapter 3 The male–female earnings differential in Britain

1 For a fuller discussion of this topic, with further supporting evidence, see P. J. Sloane, *The Earnings Gap between Men and Women in Britain: The Current State of Research Knowledge,* Equal Opportunities Commission/Social Science Research Council Joint Panel on Equal Opportunities Research, Social Science Research Council, London, 1981.
2 For an excellent survey see J. R. Moroney, 'Do Women Earn Less Under Capitalism?', *Economic Journal,* Vol. 88, No. 352, December 1978.
3 *The Economic Role of Women in the ECE Region,* United Nations, New York, 1980.
4 One attempt to test for the effects of government policy in this area suggested a significant shift in the relationship to the extent of eight percentage points. This study used a regression model in which relative male–female earnings are explained by unemployment, a dummy for the impact of legislation, an incremental time trend and time. However, it appeared that equal pay as such was less important than flat-rate incomes policies in moderating the position of women. See B. Chiplin, M. M. Curran and C. J. Parsley, 'Relative Female Earnings in Great Britain and the Impact of Legislation', in P. J. Sloane, ed., *Women and Low Pay,* Macmillan, London, 1980.
5 *Employment Gazette,* Vol. 88, No. 10, October, 1980, H.M.S.O.
6 *E. O. C. Research Bulletin,* Vol. 1, No. 1, Winter 1978–9.
7 In 1976 over 80 per cent of higher-degree graduates in the U.K. were male, though, as with the case of undergraduates, the percentage of women has been increasing in recent years.
8 Catherine Hakim, *Occupational Segregation: A Comparative Study of the Degree and Pattern of the Differentiation between Men and Women's Work in Britain, the United States and other countries,* Research Paper No. 9, Department of Employment, November 1979.
9 The tendency for women to be concentrated in relatively few occupations has been referred to in the literature as the 'crowding hypothesis'. The effect of a greater number of persons being attracted into a particular occupation is to depress wages there, relative to those found in other occupations. Further, to the extent that barriers to mobility exist between this and other occupations there will be no tendency for any such wage

difference to be eliminated by the forces of competition in the long run. This 'crowding hypothesis' has much in common with the notion of a dual labour market. That is, certain jobs are held to possess favourable attributes such as high pay, pleasant working conditions, possibilities for training and promotion and job security, whilst others possess unfavourable attributes, such as low pay, harsh working conditions, no possibilities for upward advancement and job insecurity. It is held that women are more than proportionately found in the latter type of job.

10 B. Chiplin and P. J. Sloane, *Sex Discrimination in the Labour Market*, Macmillan, London, 1976.

11 Christine Greenhalgh, 'Male–Female Wage Differentials in Great Britain: Is Marriage an Equal Opportunity?' *Economic Journal*, Vol. 90, No. 360, December 1980.

12 Married women's propensity to participate in the labour force will be influenced not only by the number and age of children but also by the adequacy of child-care facilities. According to the General Household Survey in 1976 approximately one-third of women who stayed at home and cared for children said they would go back to work earlier if satisfactory child-care arrangements could be made.

13 Greenhalgh, 'Male–Female Wage Differentials in Great Britain.'

14 W. S. Siebert and P. J. Sloane, 'The Measurement of Sex and Marital Status Discrimination at the Workplace', *Economica*, Vol. 48, May 1981.

15 It should be noted that these are cross-section rather than time-series results, so that it could not necessarily be inferred that for any individual earnings will actually decline after a certain age.

16 The participation rate for all working age women is lowest in the age group 25–34, despite the fact that this is the highest age participation rate for non-married women. Unfortunately the New Earnings Survey data do not distinguish marital status, so that it is not possible to construct age–earnings profiles separately for married and for single women.

17 See for instance R. Tsuchigane and N. Dodge, *Economic Discrimination Against Women in the United States: Measures and Changes*, Lexington Books, Lexington, Mass. 1974.
Another example is top-class sporting activity. Though the gap between the sexes has been diminishing, Olympic records suggest a 10 per cent performance differential by men over women.

18 Since men work longer hours than women (not only because of overtime working but also because hours are on average longer for men who are relatively concentrated in manual occupations) the male–female hourly wage differential is smaller than its weekly equivalent.

19 Source: Equal Opportunities Commission, *Fourth Annual Report*, 1979.

20 For a detailed analysis of collective bargaining coverage by sex see M. B. Gregory and A. W. J. Thomson, 'Trade Union Coverage, Mark-up

Bargaining Structure and Earnings in Britain, 1973 and 1978', *British Journal of Industrial Relations*, Vol. xix, No. 1, March 1981.
21 S. Nickell, 'Trade Unions and the Position of Women in the Industrial Wages Structure,' *British Journal of Industrial Relations*, Vol. xv, No. 2, July 1977.

Chapter 4 Monitoring discrimination and the law

1 E.O.C., *Third Annual Report*, 1978.
2 *The Annual Report of the Equal Opportunities Commission*, 1976.
3 *ibid.*
4 This Code is, at the time of writing (1981), being circulated for comments among employers, trade unions and other interested bodies. The final form, which will be presented to the Secretary of State for Employment to lay before Parliament for approval, may differ with respect to the references made in this chapter. The draft Code recognises that some of the references may be inappropriate for small firms where recruitment, selection and training are not delegated to specialist staff.
5 E.O.C., *Equality between the Sexes in Industry: How far have we come?*, 1978.
6 E.O.C., *Guidance on Equal Opportunities Policies and Practices in Employment*, 1978.
7 On this point, see, for example, the authors' *Sex Discrimination in the Labour Market*, Macmillan, London, 1976, Chapter 7 and R. C. Battalio, J. H. Kagel and M. O. Reynolds, 'A Note on the Distribution of Earnings and Output in an Experimental Economy', *Economic Journal*, Vol. 88, No. 352, December, 1978.
8 Indeed, certain sections of the draft Code, if implemented, would tend to raise the costs of labour, reducing employment opportunities for all, and some would increase the costs of female labour relative to male. For instance the Code suggests that consideration be given where practicable to allowing jobs to be carried out on a flexible basis (e.g. flexible working hours, part-time work and job sharing); to the introduction of child-care facilities for employees; to personal leave agreements to cover situations where dependants are ill; and to improving on statutory maternity provisions by reducing qualifying periods and lengthening periods of paid leave. Overall, these are likely to increase the relative costs of employing women; and if implemented this is likely to be only partially offset by the proposal that there should be paternity as well as maternity leave.
9 For a further discussion of this concept see Chapter 5.
10 On this see R. S. Goldfarb and J. R. Hosek, 'Explaining Male–Female Wage Differentials for the Same Job', *Journal of Human Resources*, Vol. xi, No. 1, Winter 1976.

11 I.P.M. Joint Standing Committee on Discrimination, *Towards Fairer Selection: A Code for Non-Discrimination*, I.P.M. 1978. The E.O.C. draft Code of Practice also suggests that if the policies and procedures outlined are implemented they may avoid liability for employees' discriminatory acts in any proceedings brought against them. However, employers should avoid the danger that over-zealous attempts at positive equal opportunities may lead to reverse discrimination.

12 The investigation into Electrolux followed a recommendation in an E.A.T. decision. The first part of the investigation into equal pay has been completed and the first non-discrimination notice issued. The E.O.C. advised the company on the formulation of a non-discriminatory job-evaluation scheme which resulted in a new grading structure and this is being monitored. A report on the sex discrimination aspects of the investigation is awaited. The other four investigations are regarded as having wider implications than the specific areas of employment investigated. Thus, the Coventry and North Gwent investigations both relate to the question of teaching appointments and the promotion of female teachers to senior posts; the Leeds Permanent Building Society investigation concerns certain employment practices relating to recruitment, training and promotion in another area where female employment is important; and the investigation into a printing trade union (S.O.G.A.T.) relates to an allegation that in two London branches membership conditions led to the restriction of women to less favourable employment opportunities than their male counterparts, and that pressure was exerted on employees to discriminate.

13 For a complete analysis see the articles entitled 'Equal Pay and Sex Discrimination', *Department of Employment Gazette*, in the April issue of 1977, 1978, 1979 and 1980, and the May issue of 1981.

14 Two other cases of this type have been referred to the E.C.J. In *Garland v. British Rail Engineering* a provision for travel concessions for employees, their wives and children was extended after retirement for men but in the case of women was restricted after retirement to the women themselves. The Court of Appeal held that this was excluded by the provisions in the legislation concerning death or retirement, but the House of Lords referred it to the European Court. In a second case, *Burton v. British Railways Board*, where a policy of early redundancy was applied to men aged 60 and over and women aged 55 and over, a 58-year-old man whose application was rejected claimed unfair discrimination and E.A.T. referred this also to the E.C.J.

15 In its draft Code of Practice the E.O.C. suggests that part-time workers should receive pay and other benefits on a *pro rata* basis to full-time employees.

16 U.S. case law may also be relevant. In *Meeks v. National Union of*

Agricultural Workers the industrial tribunal chairman noted the relevance of u.s. case law to cases of indirect discrimination in Britain, referring to the use of statistics and job-relevant criteria in *Griggs v. Duke Power Co.* For a discussion of North American legislation see H. C. Jain and P. J. Sloane, 'Race, Sex and Minority Group Discrimination Legislation in North America and Britain,' *Industrial Relations Journal*, Vol. 9, No. 2, Summer 1978; Janet S. Goodman and Virginia Novarra, 'The Sex Discrimination Act 1975 – File and Forget', *Personnel Review*, Vol. 17, No. 1, Winter 1978 and Pauline Glucklich and Margery Povall, 'Equal Opportunities: A Case for Action in Default of the Law', *Personnel Management*, January 1979. For a comparison of North American and British legislation see also H. C. Jain and P. J. Sloane, *Equal Employment Issues*, Praeger, New York, 1981.

17 The e.o.c.'s draft Code of Practice also suggests analyses should be undertaken of transfers, promotions, job offers, the extent of participation in training and development activities and, where possible, the use of grievance procedures in relation to equal opportunities.

18 Choice of variables will be heavily influenced by the variables thought by management explicitly or implicitly to influence pay and progress within the firm. The law itself does not specify what these should be, merely that they should be reasonable in the context of the job. What is essential is that such variables should be applied to each sex/marital status group equally.

19 For fuller details see i.d.s. Handbook No. 14, *Equal Pay, Sex Discrimination, Maternity Rights*, Income Data Services, September, 1979.

20 For a fuller discussion of this question see H. C. Jain and P. J. Sloane, 'Minority Workers, The Structure of Labour Markets and Anti-Discrimination Legislation', *International Journal of Social Economics*, Vol. 7, No. 3, 1980; and the same authors, *Equal Employment Issues*.

21 K. Mayhew, 'Earnings Dispersion in Local Labour Markets: Implications for Search Behaviour', *Oxford Bulletin of Economics and Statistics*, May, 1977 In general for unskilled workers the proportion of total dispersion accounted for by intra-plant differences in earnings varies from 1.8 per cent to 85.3 per cent, with a median observation of 26.2 per cent. For the semi-skilled group (which is likely to be more heterogeneous) the intra-plant dispersion is greater, ranging from 17.7 per cent to 93.1 per cent, with a median observation of 65.4 per cent. Whilst payment-by-results systems cause the intra-plant dispersion of earnings to rise as one might expect, the effect is apparently not all that great.

22 Similar questions have arisen over the question of where individuals should be placed on incremental pay scales. See *Pointon v. University of Sussex* and *Grundy v. University of Keele and Greenwood.* In the latter

case it was decided that it was unlawful to overlook the candidate for upgrading because, as a married woman with three young children and a husband who lectured at the University, she was not likely to leave over dissatisfaction with pay, unlike the other male computing assistants.

23 I.P.M. report, *Towards Fairer Selection*.

24 E.O.C. *Guidance on Equal Opportunities*. The E.O.C. also suggests that whilst it is lawful to discriminate against single persons it is good employment practice to treat this group in the same way as married persons.

25 Any condition applied must be *necessary*. See *Steel v. Union of Post Office Workers and the Post Office*.

26 I.P.M. report, *Towards Fairer Selection*.

27 See S. Rearden, 'A Fair Share of Talent: Scholarships for Girls as Engineering Technicians', *Department of Employment Gazette*, February 1979.

28 See P. Glucklich, M. Povall, M. W. Snell and A. Zell, 'Equal Pay and Opportunity', *Department of Employment Gazette*, July, 1978.

29 The E.O.C. Code suggests that where an organisation operates an appraisal system for promotion, records should be kept and monitored. In particular, care should be taken to avoid unduly restrictive age limits in relation to training. Further, it is suggested that a requirement for unbroken lengths of service or promotion on the basis of seniority by itself could amount to unlawful indirect discrimination.

30 P. Glucklich and M. Povall, 'Equal Opportunities'.

31 It should be pointed out that E.A.T. has confirmed that in the case of indirect discrimination the onus of proof is on the employer to show that the requirement is justifiable.

32 Details were not provided in 29 per cent of cases.

33 National Board for Prices and Incomes, *Job Evaluation*, Report No. 83, H.M.S.O. 1968.

34 A.C.A.S., *Job Evaluation*, Advisory Booklet No. 1, undated.

35 *ibid*.

36 'Job Evaluation – Part 2: Making the Evaluations', *Industrial Relations Review and Report*, No. 250, June 1981.

37 H. Carty, 'The Question of Motive in Discrimination', *New Law Journal*, 3 July 1980 notes that the concept of detriment is a troublesome one. In the Jeremiah case Lord Denning simply states that the requirement to work in dirty conditions is a detriment. Brandon, L. J. believed that regard must be paid to the fact that additional payment was received by the men, suggesting that dirty work and extra payments have to be balanced against each other before one can decide whether one sex is disadvantaged.

38 The difficulties of the less favourable treatment test also arose in *Skyrail Oceanic Ltd v. Coleman*. A married woman was dismissed after she

married the employee of a rival. E.A.T. found the tribunal had adopted the wrong approach in comparing the woman's treatment with that of her husband who was employed by a *different* company. The essential question is whether the allegedly discriminatory employer has treated a woman less favourably than he has or would have treated one of his *own* male employees.

39 Though this may be unfair dismissal under the Employment Protection (Consolidation) Act, complainants are more likely to use unfair dismissal provisions under such circumstances so long as the requirement of 52 weeks' service has been met.

40 As the draft Code of Practice notes, we should also bear in mind that as an employer a trade union has the same responsibilities for equality of opportunity as any other employer.

Chapter 5 Measuring discrimination at the place of work

1 R. Higgs, 'Firm-specific Evidence on Racial Wage Differentials and Workforce Segregation', *American Economic Review*, Vol. 67, 1977, pp. 236–45.

2 For an interesting analysis of the problem see also M. Manser and M. Brown, 'Bargaining Analyses of Household Decisions' in Cynthia B. Lloyd, Emily S. Andrews and Curtis L. Gilroy, *Women in the Labour Market*, Columbia University Press, 1979.

3 See e.g., G. E. Johnson and F. P. Stafford, 'The Earnings and Promotion of Women Faculty', *American Economic Review*, Vol. 64, 1974, pp. 888–903; and M. H. Strober and A. O. Quester, 'The Earnings and Promotions of Women Faculty: Comment', *American Economic Review*, Vol. 67, 1977, pp. 207–13.

4 For recent work in a U.K. context see Catherine Hakim, *Occupational Segregation: A Comparative Study of the Degree and Pattern of the Differentiation Between Men and Women's Work in Britain, the United States and Other Countries'*, Research Paper No. 9, Department of Employment, November 1979

5 For such an approach in the U.S. see R. J. Flanagan, 'Actual versus Potential Impact of Government Antidiscrimination Programmes', *Industrial and Labor Relations Review*, Vol. 29, No. 4, 1976; pp. 486–507.

6 Dennis J. Aigner and Glen G. Cain, 'Statistical Theories of Discrimination in Labour Markets', *Industrial and Labor Relations Review*, Vol. 30, No. 2, 1977, pp. 175–87.

7 W. Y. Oi, 'Labour as a Quasi-fixed Factor', *Journal of Political Economy*, Vol. 70, 1962, pp. 538–55.

8 An alternative view to that of the human-capital school discussed in the

next chapter is that education merely signals the innate productive ability of the individual without enhancing it. See e.g., K. J. Arrow, 'Higher Education as a Filter', *Journal of Public Economics*, Vol. 2, 1973, pp. 193–216; J. E. Stiglitz, 'The Theory of Screening, Education and the Distribution of Income', *American Economic Review*, Vol. 65, 1975, pp. 282–300 and R. Layard and G. Psacharopoulos, 'The Screening Hypothesis and the Social Returns to Education', *Journal of Political Economy*, Vol. 82, 1974, pp. 985–98.

9 See for instance, G. R. Ghez and G. S. Becker, *The Allocation of Time and Goods Over the Life Cycle*, National Bureau of Economic Research, 1975.

10 For a full derivation, see Jacob Mincer, *Schooling, Experience and Earnings*, National Bureau of Economic Research, Columbia University Press, 1974. For a clear statement of the necessary assumptions see A. S. Blinder, 'On Dogmatism in Human Capital Theory', *Journal of Human Resources*, Vol. 11, 1976, pp. 9–22.

11 See Jacob Mincer, 'Progress in Human Capital Analyses of the Distribution of Earnings', in A. B. Atkinson (ed.), *Studies in the Personal Distribution of Earnings*, Allen and Unwin, 1976. For a pathbreaking analysis relating to women see J. Mincer and S. Polachek, 'Family Investments in Human Capital: Earnings of Women', *Journal of Political Economy*, Vol. 82, 1974, pp. s76–108.

12 Z. Griliches, 'Estimating the Returns to Schooling: Some Econometric Problems', *Econometrica*, Vol. 45, 1977, pp. 1–22; G. Chamberlain, 'Education, Income and Ability Re-visited', *Journal of Econometrics*, Vol. 5, 1977, pp. 241–57.

13 Z. Griliches, 'Estimating the Returns to Schooling'.

14 G. S. Becker, *Human Capital*, 2nd edn, National Bureau of Economic Research, 1975. For an application to the U.K. see Dennis Lees and Brian Chiplin, 'The Economics of Industrial Training', *Lloyds Bank Review*, April 1970, pp. 29–41.

15 For a discussion of the use of dummy variables see any textbook in econometrics such as J. Johnston, *Econometric Methods*, 2nd edn, McGraw-Hill, 1972, pp. 176–86.

16 R. Oaxaca, 'Male–Female Wage Differentials in Urban Labour Markets', *International Economic Review*, 1973.

17 See for instance, G. S. Maddala, *Econometrics*, McGraw-Hill, New York, 1977, pp. 155–7.

18 See Brian Chiplin, 'The Effect of Omitted Variables on the Measurement of Discrimination', Department of Industrial Economics, University of Nottingham, Discussion Paper No. 69, 1979, mimeo.

19 J. Mincer and S. Polachek, 'Family Investments in Human Capital: Earnings of Women', *Journal of Political Economy*, Vol. 82, 1974, pp. s76–108.

20 W. S. Siebert and P. J. Sloane, 'The Measurement of Sex and Marital Status Discrimination at the Workplace', *Economica*, Vol. 48, May 1981; C. Greenhalgh, 'Male–Female Wage Differentials in Great Britain: Is Marriage an Equal Opportunity?', *Economic Journal*, Vol. 90, No. 360, December 1980.

21 C. Greenhalgh, 'Male–Female Wage Differentials in Great Britain'.

22 See M. Manser and M. Brown, 'Bargaining Analyses of Household Decisions', for an interesting exploration of the problem.

23 B. Chiplin and P. J. Sloane, 'Personal Characteristics and Sex Differentials in Professional Employment', *Economic Journal*, Vol. 86, 1976, pp. 729–45.

24 As their discrimination coefficient (D) Sloane and Siebert use

$$D = \frac{(\bar{F}_e/\bar{M} - \bar{F}/\bar{M})}{\bar{F}_e/\bar{M}} = 1 - \frac{\bar{F}/\bar{M}}{\bar{F}_e/\bar{M}}$$

This is equivalent to the measure D_3 (equation 5.3), i.e.

$$D_3 = \frac{\bar{M}/\bar{F} - \bar{M}/\bar{F}_e}{\bar{M}/\bar{F}}$$

Since
$$\frac{\bar{M}}{\bar{F}} = \frac{1}{\bar{F}/\bar{M}}$$

and
$$\frac{\bar{M}}{\bar{F}_e} = \frac{1}{\bar{F}_e/\bar{M}}$$

which on substitution gives:

$$D = \frac{\dfrac{1}{\bar{F}/\bar{M}} - \dfrac{1}{\bar{F}_e/\bar{M}}}{\dfrac{1}{\bar{F}/\bar{M}}} = 1 - \frac{\bar{F}/\bar{M}}{\bar{F}_e/\bar{M}}$$

25 C. Greenhalgh, 'Male–Female Wage Differentials in Great Britain'.

26 G. S. Chow, 'Tests of Equality Between Subsets of Coefficients in Two Linear Regressions', *Econometrica*, Vol. 28, 1960, pp. 591–605. For a clear explanation see, e.g. G. S. Maddala, *Econometrics*, McGraw-Hill 1977.

27 Gary S. Becker, *The Economics of Discrimination*, 2nd edn, University of Chicago Press, 1971.

28 J. A. Boulet and J. C. R. Rowley, 'Measurement of Discrimination in the Labour Market: A Comment', *Canadian Journal of Economics*, Vol. 10, 1977, pp. 149–54.

29 Becker, *Economics of Discrimination.*
30 S. H. Masters, 'Measurements of Discrimination in the Labour Market: Reply', *Canadian Journal of Economics*, Vol. 10, 1977, pp. 154–5.
31 C. Greenhalgh, Male–Female Wage Differentials in Great Britain'.
32 See, for example, T. Yamane, *Statistics: an Introductory Analysis*, 2nd edn, Harper and Row, New York, 1967, pp. 299–304.

Chapter 6 The recruitment of labour

1 See A. Michael Spence, *Market Signaling: Informational Transfer in Hiring and Related Screening Processes*, Harvard University Press, Cambridge, Mass. 1974.
2 It was felt appropriate to conduct such a study in a comparatively tight labour market (East Midlands) and a comparatively slack one (West of Scotland) since it has been hypothesised that as labour markets tighten employers will consider the employment of groups previously excluded on the basis of cheap screens. Hence we might expect the degree of sex segregation to be less marked in the East Midlands than in the West of Scotland.
3 The time periods chosen were partly a function of the availability of data, but the fact that the time periods were different in the two cases is not felt to be sufficiently important to invalidate the comparison.
4 The Job Centre chosen in the West of Scotland tends to experience a rather lower than average level of unemployment for the West of Scotland as a whole but rather higher than the average for Great Britain as a whole.
5 In two cases men were sent for interview where typing was a job requirement, whilst three women were sent for interview where apprenticeship was a requirement, two being appointed.
6 This fall is statistically significant ($t = 3.81$).
7 Reference back to Table 6.2 reveals that this figure is very much higher than a year or so earlier, so that we are observing a trend over a period of more than twelve months, and there may have been some anticipation of the legislation or more fundamental forces at work.
8 For a regression analysis of these effects see Appendix 6.2.
9 Whilst it is dangerous to generalise from a range of highly individual responses it does appear that the reasons advanced for female preference are more negative than those for male preference; they focus to a greater extent on the reasons why men *would not do* the job rather than on reasons why women are intrinsically well suited to it. In the case of male preference the focus is on the reasons why women *are not suited to the job* rather than the reasons why they would not do it if given the opportunity.
10 This section is based on Brian Chiplin, 'An Alternative Approach to the

Measurement of Sex Discrimination: An Illustration from University Entrance', *Economic Journal*, December 1981.
11 Variables reflecting other preferences were included but in all cases proved insignificant.
12 See D. McFadden, 'Conditional Logit Analysis of Qualitative Choice Behaviour', in P. Zarembka (ed.) *Frontiers in Econometrics*, Academic Press, 1973.
13 See M. Nerlove and S. J. Press, *Univariate and Multivariate Log-Linear and Logistic Models*, Report No. R-1306-EDA/MIH, Rand Corporation, 1973.
14 D. McFadden, 'Conditional Logit Analysis of Qualitative Choice Behaviour'.

Chapter 7 Conclusions

1 Catherine Hakim, *Occupational Segregation: A Comparative Study of the Degree and Pattern of the Differentiation Between Men and Women's work in Britain, the United States and Other Countries*, Research Paper No. 9, Department of Employment, November 1979.
2 Equal Opportunities Commission, *Fifth Annual Report*, 1980, H.M.S.O.
3 See e.g. C. K. Rowley, 'Social Sciences and Law: The Relevance of Economic Theories', *Oxford Journal of Legal Studies*, No. 3, 1981.
4 W. S. Siebert and P. J. Sloane, 'The Measurement of Sex and Marital Status Discrimination at the Workplace', *Economica*, Vol. 48, No. 190, May 1981, pp. 125–42.
5 M. W. Snell, P. Glucklich, and M. Povall, *Equal Pay and Opportunities: A Study of the Implementation and Effects of the Equal Pay and Sex Discrimination Acts in 26 Organisations*, Research Paper No. 20, Department of Employment, April 1981.

Other publications associated with the project

1. B. Chiplin 'Non Convexity of Indifference Surfaces in the Case of Labour Market Discrimination', *American Economic Review*, December 1976
2. B. Chiplin 'Sexual Discrimination: Are There Any Lessons from Criminal Behaviour?', *Applied Economics*, December 1976
3. B. Chiplin 'An Evaluation of Sex Discrimination: Some Problems and a Suggested Re-orientation', in C. B. Lloyd, E. S. Andrews, and C. L. Gilroy, *Women in the Labour Market*, Columbia University Press, 1979
4. B. Chiplin 'An Alternative Approach to the Measurement of Sex Discrimination: An Illustration From University Entrance', *Economic Journal*, December 1981
5. B. Chiplin, M. M. Curran and C. J. Parsley 'Relative Female Earnings in Great Britain and the Impact of Legislation', in Peter J. Sloane, ed., *Women and Low Pay*, Macmillan, 1980
6. B. Chiplin and P. J. Sloane 'Sexual Discrimination in the Labour Market', *British Journal of Industrial Relations*, November 1974, reprinted in Alice H. Amsden, ed., *The Economics of Women and Work*, Penguin Books, 1980
7. B. Chiplin and P. J. Sloane 'Equal Employment Opportunities for Women', *Industrial Relations Journal*, Autumn 1975
8. B. Chiplin and P. J. Sloane 'Equal Pay in Great Britain', in B. O. Pettman, ed., *Equal Pay for Women*, MCB Publications, 1975.
9. B. Chiplin and P. J. Sloane 'Male–Female Earnings Differences: A Further Analysis', *British Journal of Industrial Relations*, March 1976
10. B. Chiplin and P. J. Sloane *Sex Discrimination in the Labour Market*, Macmillan, 1976
11. B. Chiplin and P. J. Sloane 'Personal Characteristics and Sex Differentials in Professional Employment', *Economic Journal*, December 1976
12. P. J. Sloane *The Earnings Gap between Men and Women in Britain*, Social Science Research Council/Equal Opportunities Commission, London, 1981

13. P. J. Sloane 'Discrimination in the Labour Market: A Survey of Theory and Evidence', in M. Summer, ed., *Surveys of Economic Theory*, Longman, forthcoming
14. P. J. Sloane (with H. C. Jain) 'Race, Sex and Minority Group Discrimination Legislation in North America and Britain', *Industrial Relations Journal*, Summer 1978
15. P. J. Sloane (with H. C. Jain) 'Minority Workers, the Structure of Labour Markets and Anti-Discrimination Legislation', *International Journal of Social Economics*, Vol. 7, No. 3, 1980
16. P. J. Sloane (with H. C. Jain) *Equal Employment Issues*, Praeger, 1981
17. P. J. Sloane and W. S. Siebert 'Low Pay Amongst Women: The Facts' in P. J. Sloane, ed., *Women and Low Pay*
18. W. S. Siebert and P. J. Sloane 'Shortcomings and Problems in Analyses of Women and Low Pay', in P. J. Sloane, ed., *Women and Low Pay*
19. W. S. Siebert and P. J. Sloane 'The Measurement of Sex and Marital Status Discrimination at the Workplace', *Economica*, Vol. 48, May 1981

Author index

149

Author index

Medoff, M. H., 134, 135
Mincer, J., 10, 69, 134, 143
Moroney, J. R., 136
Morris, D. J., 135

Neimi, B. T., 133
Nerlove, M., 146
Nickell, S., 138
Novarra, V., 140

Oaxaca, R., 66, 67, 143
Oi, W. Y., 142
Oster, S. M., 135

Papps, I., 18, 135
Parsley, C. J., 136, 147
Polachek, S., 10, 69, 134, 143
Povall, M., 48, 129, 135, 140, 141, 146
Press, S. J., 146
Psacharopoulos, G., 143

Quester, A. O., 142

Rearden, S., 141
Reynolds, M. O., 60, 133, 138
Roemer, J. E., 135
Rowley, C. K., 8, 134, 146
Rowley, J. C. R., 85, 144

Sawhill, I. V., 136
Shepherd, W. G., 134
Siebert, W. S., 28, 79, 133, 137, 144, 146, 148
Sloane, P. J., 28, 72, 73, 79, 128, 133, 136, 137, 140, 144, 146, 147, 148
Snell, M. W., 129, 135, 141, 146
Sowell, T., 133
Spence, A. M., 145
Stafford, F. P., 142
Stiglitz, J. E., 7, 133, 143
Strober, M. H., 142

Tanzer, M., 134
Thomson, A. W. J., 137
Thurow, L. C., 133, 135
Trapani, J. M., 135
Tsuchigane, R., 137
Turnbull, P., 134

Wallace, P. A. (ed.), 133, 134, 136
Williams, G., 134

Yamane, T., 145

Zarembka, P. (ed.), 146
Zell, A., 141

150

General index

Advisory Conciliation and Arbitration Service (A.C.A.S.)
  job evaluation, 52, 141 n34 and 5
affirmative action, 1, 16, 19, 42, 129
age
  earnings, 28–9, 30, 50
  human capital investment, 62
  legislation, 50
  recruitment, 46, 93
  retirement, 55
Atkin Committee: output by women, 30

bargaining, 12–13, 31–2, 130, 137 n20
blue-collar workers, 9
Brandon, L. J., 141 n37
British Employment Gazette
  New Earnings Survey, 24

careers
  dual labour markets, 13
  of graduates, 25
  legislation, 19
  marital status, 28, 41, 123
  overtime, 47, 48
  promotion, 37, 41, 47–8, 55
  shift-work, 47
  see also occupational segregation
Central Arbitration Committee, 55
  job evaluation, 15, 52
children, *see* families
Chow test, 82, 144 n26
Civil Rights Act, Title VII, 20
Civil Service, 125
Commission for Racial Equality
  on recruitment methods, 45
cost minimisation, 6, 7
Court of Appeal, 35, 38, 44, 53, 54
Coventry and North Gwent
    investigation, 139 n12

crowding hypothesis, 13, 136–7 n9

Denning, Lord, 44, 54, 141 n37
Department of Education and Science (D.E.S.)
  day-release courses, 26
Department of Employment, 27, 55, 139 n13
D.E.S., *see* Department of Education and Science
detriment, concept of, 53–4, 141 n37–9
discrimination
  age, 46, 93
  definitions, 4–8
  direct, 15, 37, 40, 54
  dismissal, 53
  dual labour markets, 13, 99, 137 n9
  existence and extent, 60–1
  identification methods (universities), 107–10, 119, 121
  indirect, 15–16, 34, 37, 39, 40, 46, 48, 54, 130, 141 n29
  job levels, 59
  measurement of, 63–8, 81–6, 108–121, 137 n14; marital status in, 70–2, 74–5, 78–9, 80, 124; selection of variables for, 68–9, 109–15, 140 n18
  and non-discrimination notices, 16
  and prejudice 5
  promotion, 101–2
  racial, 5, 6, 14, 19, 35–6
  redundancy, 139 n14
  reverse, 16, 69, 129
  screening for recruitment, 87, 88
  selection bias (university entrance), 104–16
  sexual, 16–21, 72–86
  taste for, 5, 8–9, 11–12, 60

151

General index

theories, 8–14
vacancy specifications, 93–8, 100–1
see also earnings differentials
dismissal, 53, 141–2 n38 and 9
and legislation, 37
divide-and-conquer strategy, 14
dual labour markets, 13, 99, 137 n9

earnings differentials, 1–2, 6, 22–3, 93, 122
absence from work, 11, 18–19, 30, 63
age-related, 28–9, 30, 50
crowding hypothesis, 19, 24–5, 74
education, 19, 24–6
effects of children, 28, 71
experience-related, 19, 28–9
inter- and intra-plant, 43–4, 140 n21
length of service, 74, 76–7
local labour markets, 43–4
manual and non-manual workers, 22–3, 29, 30, 31
marginal productivity, 60–1, 85
marital status, 9–10, 27–8, 42–3, 71, 74–5, 78–9, 80, 124
measurements of, 65–8
occupations, 26–7
overtime, 31, 40, 50, 58, 137 n18
payment-by-results, 31, 40, 50, 58
piece-rate, 30
prediction, in event of role-reversal, 131
productivity, 6, 29, 30, 61
reasons for, 2–3, 10, 24–32, 58–60, 64
recruitment, 93, 98, 104
reflection of discrimination, 125
seniority, 58
sex, 72–86, 93
shift-work, 31, 50, 58
skills, 35, 58
trades unions, 24, 31–2
training, 19, 20, 24–6
United States, 1–2, 19–20, 22, 23, 59
universities, 59
worldwide occurrence, 22–3
see also Equal Pay Act
earnings functions, 33, 40
estimation of, 61, 64–9
and human capital, 61–2
interpretation, 68–72
measurement of discrimination, 82–6
sex discrimination, 72–4, 76–7

E.A.T., *see* Employment Appeals Tribunal
E.C.J., *see* European Court of Justice
economists
approach to discrimination, 4, 7–9, 13–14, 59, 127
on market imperfections, 88
education
before employment, 2, 7, 24, 25
and earnings, 19, 24–5, 74, 76–7
human capital investment, 62–3
opportunities to receive, 2–3
and rate-of-return estimates, 25
see also training; university entrance
Electrolux Ltd, 36, 139 n12
employers
and absenteeism, 34–5
discrimination by, 9, 12, 47, 58
hiring practices, 6–7, 88, 93–8, 100–4, 124
and legislation, 16, 34, 35, 36, 125–6, 128, 129–30
paternalistic attitudes, 28
provision of training, 26
Employment Appeals Tribunal (E.A.T.)
detrimental acts and dismissal, 53–4
interviews, 46
job evaluation, 51
'like' work, 48
market forces, 44
racial discrimination, 35–6
seniority, 48
skills in labour market, 43
times at work, 49–50
Employment Protection Act, 18, 142 n39
Employment Services Agency (E.S.A.), 88, 89
Engineering Industry Training Board, 47, 141 n27
E.O.C., *see* Equal Opportunities Commission
E.P.A., *see* Equal Pay Act
Equal Employment Opportunity Title, 20
Equal Opportunities Commission (E.O.C.), 1, 16, 59, 137 n19, 138 n5 and 6
education, 25
formal investigations by, 36
implementation of policies, 34, 39–44
job evaluation, 50, 52, 55

General index

level of pay, 48–53
and promotion, 47–8
recruitment, 44–7
role of, 129–32
sex discrimination, 16–21, 36–7
see also individual Acts; legal cases
litigation, costs of, 36
London School of Economics
Equal Pay and Opportunity Project, 47

marital status
careers, 28, 41, 123
earnings, 28, 42–3
jobs: horizons, 9, 10, 28; and mobility, 9, 27, 42–3
labour force participation, 10, 27, 122
labour markets, 9–10, 28, 70
in measurements of discrimination, 70–2, 74–5, 78–9, 80, 124
motivation to work, 70
role specialisation, 10, 28, 41, 122; reverse r.s., 131
Sex Discrimination Act, 27, 127
view of work, 41
market power, 12
maternity leave provisions, 18, 138 n8
micro-technology, 21
monopoly power models, 12–13
monopsony, 133 n7

National Board for Prices and Incomes
job evaluation, 141 n33
New Earnings Survey (N.E.S.), 23–4
differential earnings, 29–31, 137 n16
New York (conference), 19–20

occupational licensing, 13
occupational segregation
by gender, 90–2
horizontal, 26, 59
vertical, 26–7, 59
omitted-variable bias, 68–9

Paasche price index, 84
pay, see earnings differentials
pay structure
and Equal Opportunities Commission, 55
incremental, 11, 27, 58
pension schemes, 38, 55
productivity, 2, 6, 40

differentials, 18, 29–30
and human capital, 61–3
marginal-, 60–1, 85
measurement of, 60
profit maximisation, 12, 14, 36
promotion, 3, 47–8
Equal Opportunities Commission, 55
and legislation, 37
prospects at interviews, 101–2
reflection of current attitudes, 125
by seniority, 48

quit rates, 30
quotas, 42, 129

rate-of-return estimates, 25
recession, 20, 126
recruitment, 3, 6–7
advertisments, 44, 45, 87
age, 46, 93
clerical vacancies, 45–6, 89, 99–104
employers specifications, 93–8
equality of opportunity, 43, 55
job descriptions, 87
legislation, 44–7
methods, 43, 44–6
pay offered, 93, 98, 104
reflection of current attitudes, 125
screening by gender, 45, 87, 88, 145 n2
Sex Discrimination Act, 93, 94, 95–8
working time specifications, 93, 98
see also interviews; jobs; vacancies
redundancy, 53–4, 139 n14

screening by gender: recruitment, 45, 87, 88, 145 n2
S.D.A., see Sex Discrimination Act
seniority
and earnings, 58
of women, 46, 48
service, length of, 11, 27, 131
and earnings, 50, 74, 76–7
Sex Discrimination Act (S.D.A.), 1, 54, 57, 59, 89, 124
burden of evidence, 55
burden of proof, 16
direct discrimination, 40
dismissal, 53–4
and employers (Section 74), 35
family status, 55
indirect discrimination, 40, 69, 130–1
and interviews, 99

155

General index

and legislation, 33, 34, 36–7, 38
marital status, 27, 127
market conditions for operation of, 124
and non-discrimination notices, 36
objectives, 15–16, 27
recruitment (Section 41 (1)), 45
redundancy, 53
training provisions, 16, 42, 47
vacancy specifications, 93, 94, 95–9
skills
  acquisition, 11, 25, 35, 122–3
  depreciation, 10–11, 123
  earnings differentials, 35, 58
  in labour market, 43, 123
  see also training
Society of Graphical and Allied Trades (S.O.G.A.T.), 139 n12
statistical analyses
  measurements of discrimination, 65–8, 81–6, 127–8; job appointees, 95, 116–18; selection of variables, 68–9, 109–15; university entrance, 108–16, 119, 121
  procedures requiring (E.O.C.), 140 n18
stereotypes
  mistaken, 35, 48
  role, 2, 46, 64, 101, 105, 116
  sex, 100, 102–3, 105
supervision, 9, 48, 100, 101, 103

teaching profession, 11
trade unions
  earnings differentials, 24, 31–2
  equality of opportunity, 39, 55, 142 n40
  female membership, 31–2
  implementation of legislation, 129–30
  job demarcation, 36
  job evaluation, 52
  restriction by monopoly power, 13, 14
  wage bills of employers, 6
training
  age limits, 141 n29
  before employment, 24–6
  during employment, 26, 63
  Equal Opportunities Commission, 34, 55–6
  general and specific, 63
  human capital investment, 62–3, 122
  offered at interviews, 94, 102

Sex Discrimination Act, 16, 42, 47
Treaty of Rome, 37
of women, 10, 35, 41, 94, 123; in engineering, 47, 105, 141 n27
see also education
Treaty of Rome, Article 119, 37, 38, 130

U.C.C.A., see Universities Central Council on Admissions
unemployment, 20
United Nations: earnings differentials study, 22–3
United States, 127, 142 n5
  earnings differentials, 1–2, 19–20, 22, 23; in universities, 59
  equal opportunities policies, 42, 43
  indirect discrimination, 16, 46, 139–40 n16
  legislation, 1, 19–20, 46, 129
  New York (conference), 19–20
  skills, 11, 123
  Standard Metropolitan Statistical Area, 43
  training, 11
Universities Central Council on Admissions (U.C.C.A.)
  statistics on entrance applications, 105, 106; selection bias study, 104–16, 119, 121
university entrance
  applications by males and females, 105, 106; places accepted, 105, 106
  qualifications, 108, 109–10, 111, 112–15
  references, 110–11, 113, 115
  selection bias study, 104–16, 119, 121; significant variables, 111–13, 115
  subject choice by males and females, 105, 107

vacancies
  clerical, 99–104, 118–19, 120
  employers specifications, 93–8
  Job Centre, 89–99, 116–18
  university entrance, 104–116, 119, 121
  see also jobs; recruitment

wage bill, maximisation, 6
wages, see earnings
white-collar workers, 9